AMERICAN COUNTRY CHRISTMAS 1994

COMPILED AND EDITED BY
Brenda Waldron Kolb
and Lelia Gray Neil

Oxmoor House®

Published by Oxmoor House, Inc., and Leisure Arts, Inc.

Library of Congress Catalog Number: 89-61909
ISBN: 0-8487-1188-2
ISSN: 1044-4904
Manufactured in the United States of America
First Printing

Editor-in-Chief: Nancy J. Fitzpatrick
Senior Homes Editor: Mary Kay Culpepper
Senior Foods Editor: Susan Carlisle Payne
Senior Editor, Editorial Services: Olivia Kindig Wells
Art Director: James Boone

AMERICAN COUNTRY CHRISTMAS 1994

Editor: Brenda Waldron Kolb
Assistant Editor: Lelia Gray Neil
Editorial Assistant: Janica Lynn York
Assistant Art Director: Cynthia R. Cooper
Copy Editor: Susan Smith Cheatham
Copy Assistants: Leslee Rester Johnson, Jennifer Mathews
Senior Photographer: John O'Hagan
Photographer: Ralph Anderson
Photostylists: Katie Stoddard, Virginia R. Cravens
Production and Distribution Manager: Phillip Lee
Associate Production Manager: Theresa L. Beste
Production Assistant: Marianne Jordan
Artist: Kelly Davis
Senior Production Designer: Larry Hunter
Publishing Systems Administrator: Rick Tucker
Recipe Development: Elizabeth Taliaferro
Test Kitchen Home Economist: Kathleen Royal
Recipe Editor: Caroline A. Grant
Recipe Copy Editor: Donna Baldone
Contributing Writers: Cecilia C. Robinson, Rebecca Meng Sommers, Heidi T. King

FRONT COVER, clockwise from top left: frame, page 8; sachet, page 12; garland, page 58; pomander, page 60; hat, page 36; gift tag, page 51.

BACK COVER, clockwise from top left: garland, page 58; pomander, page 60; fern pins, page 129; muffler, page 36; frame, page 8.

CONTENTS

DEAR READERS,

For this edition of **AMERICAN COUNTRY CHRISTMAS**, we traveled from state to state to bring you the work of some remarkably creative people.

In Ohio, we asked an artist for details on how she crafts her delicate floral masterpieces. In Pennsylvania, we photographed an expert as she plied needle and thread to make a reproduction bandbox. In Georgia, we observed a designer create a wonderful woodland tablescape. And down in Texas, we found out how a busy food editor finds time to make holiday gift giving a family affair.

We did not hesitate to look closer to home, either. From our colleagues we discovered how to piece mosaics, weave magical dried-flower wreaths, and set up a simple overdoor garland that spans the seasons. We even involved our co-workers' children, both as models and as consultants on great gifts for the younger set.

From near and far, we searched for the best ideas, shot countless photographs, sought out the most useful information. Back in our kitchens, we tested each recipe not once but twice. And then we put it all together in this year's AMERICAN COUNTRY CHRISTMAS.

The result, we hope you'll agree, is a rich, creative, but altogether practical guide for helping you celebrate Christmas in the very best of country style.

The Editors

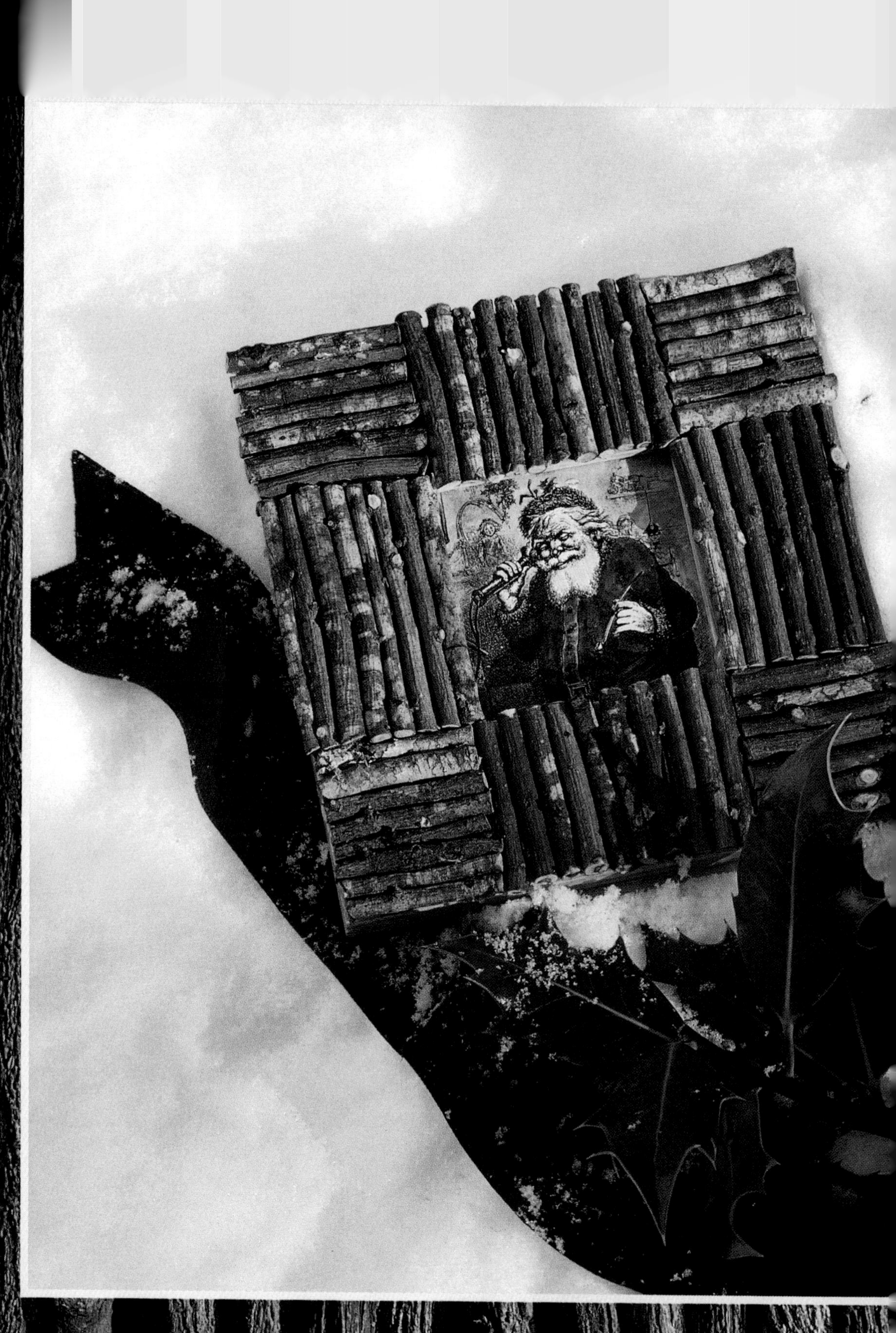

Instructions for frame are on page 9.

COUNTRY CHRISTMAS AT HOME

Picture-perfect holidays just got easier. We've done all the legwork for you, offering step-by-step ideas for decking your halls in record time. Start with something simple, such as this terrific twiggy frame.

Fit to Be Framed

Make flat, unfinished frames spectacular with a little glue and such natural objects as nuts, twigs, and seashells.

Choose a simple frame with flat sides at least 1½" wide. Purchase the frame at a crafts or variety store (for a source listing, see page 156), or construct your own using canvas stretcher bars available at art supply stores. Use a silicone adhesive or a hot-glue gun and glue sticks to attach items to the frame.

A Sea of Shells

Select shells whose colors and sizes harmonize. Glue the largest shells on the corners of the frame; then fill in the sides with the smaller shells.

Tiled with Twigs

Gather a bundle of straight twigs with similar diameters to form a parquet pattern.

Measure the width of the frame sides. Using garden clippers, cut about two dozen twigs to this measurement. Referring to the photograph, glue twigs horizontally to the corners of the frame.

Measure the remaining spaces and cut twigs to fit these measurements. Glue twigs vertically to the sides of the frame.

Roundabout Ways

Coil short lengths of twine into circles and glue them to the front of the frame, overlapping them as necessary to cover the surface completely.

Cover the outside edges of the frame by wrapping them several times with a long length of twine, gluing as you go.

Rocky Road

Gather smooth, similarly colored stones, each with one relatively flat side. Glue the flat side of each stone to the frame, spacing the stones evenly. (If desired, wrap the stone at the center top of the frame in a length of jute before gluing it to the frame.)

Apply a coat of clear varnish to the frame for a soft shine.

In a Nutshell

Harvest a mix of unshelled nuts in a variety of sizes. Randomly glue them to the frame, filling in with smaller nuts as necessary to cover the surface completely. (If desired, gild some of the nuts with gold paint before gluing them to the frame.)

Seal the frame with a coat of clear varnish.

Company's Coming

From the moment visitors step into Jane and Jim Webb's log-cabin guesthouse, they feel right at home. To help you plan for holiday company, the Webbs reveal their secrets, and we add some make-ahead projects to charm your Christmas callers.

Jane and Jim Webb lavish as much attention on their guests as they did on reassembling their log-cabin guesthouse. In 1983, the Webbs dismantled the Civil War-era cabin in Pineville, Missouri, and moved it to their property in Bartlesville, Oklahoma. They then spent three years authentically restoring the cabin. Now it is a haven for their overnight visitors, who enjoy utter privacy as well as restful views of the Webbs' formal garden and the nearby woods.

Just before houseguests arrive, Jim builds a cheery fire. From personal experience, Jane knows that the feather mattress on the old rope bed guarantees sweet dreams. And the goodnight candy she puts on the pillows is always homemade.

With this kind of attention, it's no wonder that the Webbs' reputation as terrific hosts is secure. You can indulge your own guests just as well with hospitality that reflects your personal touch (for ideas, see page 15) and the simple-to-make projects that follow.

Right: In the main room of the Webbs' cabin, guests are treated to fireside meals. The evergreen-scented sachets in the center of the table make smart party favors; see page 12 for easy instructions.

Seasonal Sachets

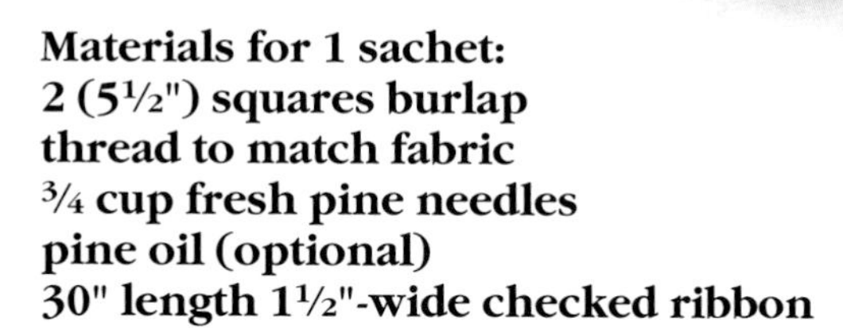

Extend a welcome with the festive scent of evergreen. Slip these pine-needle sachets in dresser drawers and closet shelves to surround your visitors with a fresh, wintry fragrance.

Materials for 1 sachet:
2 ($5\frac{1}{2}$") squares burlap
thread to match fabric
$\frac{3}{4}$ cup fresh pine needles
pine oil (optional)
30" length $1\frac{1}{2}$"-wide checked ribbon

Note: All seam allowances are $\frac{1}{4}$".

1. Zigzag burlap squares together, leaving 1 side open for turning. Clip corners and turn.

2. Fill sachet with pine needles; slipstitch opening closed. If desired, sprinkle sachet with oil for added scent. Tie ribbon in bow around sachet.

Scrunchy Holiday Hangers

Outfit closets with the fabric-covered hangers shown at left, considerate extras that are easy to make.

Materials for 1 hanger:
$\frac{1}{3}$ yard 45"-wide plaid flannel fabric
thread to match fabric
1 wire clothes hanger and pliers

Note: All seam allowances are $\frac{1}{4}$".

1. Cut 4 (3" x 45") flannel strips. With right sides facing, stitch ends of strips together. With right sides facing, fold strip in half lengthwise and stitch along long raw edge to form a tube. Turn. Turn raw edges of 1 end under and slipstitch opening closed.

2. Using pliers, untwist wire at neck of hanger. Slide flannel tube over hook end of hanger, scrunching up fabric to fit and enclosing hanger completely. Turn raw edges of tube under and slipstitch opening closed.

3. Using pliers, retwist covered wire at neck of hanger, adjusting fabric around neck and hook, and tacking fabric to secure.

Merry Mistletoe Bed Linens

Embroidered linens are a luxury, a refinement your houseguests will relish. The sheets and pillowcases pictured above can be used all year long, since their borders of stylized mistletoe leaves and berries have an appeal that's seasonless.

Materials:
pattern on page 138
tracing paper
1 set white cotton bed linens, washed and pressed
embroidery floss: dark green, green, yellow, yellow beige, peach, cream (DMC #3345, 3346, 3364, 3046, 3774, and 712 used here)

Note: For a source listing for floss, see page 156.

1. Referring to box on page 138, transfer enough pattern repeats to cover border across top edge of top sheet and front of each pillowcase.

2. Stitch design using 3 strands as indicated on pattern. (For Embroidery Diagrams, see page 55.) Remove pattern lines. Press borders with a warm iron.

Left and above: Jane and Jim's guesthouse gives overnight visitors a taste of early American country life. Many of the cabin's features, such as the wooden floors and hand-hewn logs, are original. The cozy retreat is furnished with 18th- and 19th-century American antiques as well as quilts from Jane's well-loved collection.

Coddling Your Company

Creature comforts for your overnight visitors can be as simple or lavish as you wish. Here are a few ideas for furnishing the guestroom and bath with those thoughtful touches that make guests feel pampered.

- Fill a pretty vase with fresh flowers or greenery.
- Set out a bowl of fruit and cookies for a midnight or morning snack.
- On the bedside table, provide an alarm clock or clock/radio, a carafe of water and water glass, and a small collection of books or magazines on subjects you know will pique your guests' interest.
- Pleasing aromas lift a room's ambience. In one or two well-chosen spots, place potpourri, scented candles, or the keepsake Seasonal Sachets on page 12.
- Near the desk or a comfortable chair, place a basket brimming with books, magazines, newspapers, guidebooks for your area, and stationery and pens.
- Appoint the guest bathroom with all manner of luxuries: a bath pillow and a basket of silky lotions, scented soaps, and herbal bath oils and salts; lots of lush bath towels; perhaps even a thick terry-cloth robe and scuffs. Be sure the basics are on hand, too, such as a blowdryer, emery boards, toothpaste and toothbrushes, and other frequently forgotten items.

Herbs for The Hearth

Enjoy the aroma of fresh herbs even in the heart of winter. Tie them together with colorful flowers to create a swag to hang on your mantel. Then clip off one bundle at a time to add a spicy fragrance to the crackling fire.

Materials:
fresh-cut fragrant herbs, such as rosemary, scented geranium, oregano, artemisia, sage, and thyme
fresh-cut flowers or blooming herbs, such as Mexican sage, yarrow, lamb's ears, and marigold
jute string or twine
3 purchased dried pomegranates
electric drill with 1/8" bit
large-eyed tapestry needle

1. Gather a variety of herbs together into a 2½"-diameter bundle. Add flowers to front of bundle for color. Wrap a length of string very tightly around bundle and knot to secure. Trim ends of string close to knot. Repeat to make 3 more bundles.

2. Drill hole through center (top to bottom) of each pomegranate. Set aside.

3. Cut 1½ yards of string. Thread needle with a doubled strand. Thread pomegranates on string, leaving a 5" loop below bottom pomegranate and about 5" between remaining pomegranates. Remove needle.

4. Referring to photograph at left, insert herb bundles between doubled strands of string and pull ends of string to tighten. Tie knot above top bundle to secure. Knot ends of string together to make hanger.

5. To use, clip off 1 herb bundle and carefully throw it on fire. Tie knot in string to prevent remaining bundles from slipping. Remove pomegranates and save them for another use; do not place them in fire.

All Through the House

These pretty herbal swags make great gifts, especially when you custom-create one to suit its recipient. Start with a raffia braid that you either make or buy at a crafts store. Attach a note to the finished swag to describe its use.

- **Culinary Swag** (see inset photograph at left): Tuck bundles of herbs for cooking into the braid, using thread to stitch the herbs in place if necessary. Some suitable herbs for this swag are dill, thyme, basil, parsley, marjoram, oregano, sage, bay leaves, and hot peppers, among others. Pinch off the herbs as needed.

- **Bouquet Garni Swag:** Combine dried whole marjoram and thyme, garlic cloves, peppercorns, dried onion flakes, and bay leaves in a bowl and toss. Put a few teaspoons of the mixture in the center of a 5" square of cheesecloth and tie the bundle with twine. Repeat to make several more. Attach the bundles to the braid with twine. Use bouquets garnis to flavor soups and stocks.

- **Sachet Swag:** Gather handfuls of rose petals or lavender into sachet bags made from 5" squares of organdy or cheesecloth tied with satin ribbon. Tie the sachets to the braid. Use the sachets to scent shelves and drawers.

- **Bath Bead Swag:** Tie small handfuls of bath beads into bundles as described for the sachets above and tie the bundles to the braid. Add the beads to a warm bath.

- **Herbal Tea Swag:** Tie small bundles of chamomile, mint, and other herbs for soothing teas as described for the sachets above. Include directions for brewing the teas.

Above and right: Gwen's design style comes to the fore in her clever woodland tablescape. "The best decorating suits your personality," she says, "and the easiest way to accomplish that is to use the things you already have on hand."

Natural Settings

To create a stunning centerpiece, interior designer Gwen Swann of Macon, Georgia, borrowed from the earth's foremost decorating authority—Mother Nature.

Whether designing an interior or decorating for a party, Gwen works with what's already available, because the results are often novel and personal.

Last Christmas Gwen created the decorations for a party given by clients Jean and Bill Snow. Inspired by their home's country setting, Gwen gathered items from their garden to design a centerpiece that resembled a little corner of nature.

Here, Gwen shows you how to create your own woodland tablescape. It is best built on a mesh-top, wrought-iron patio table—a great use for something that doesn't see a lot of service this time of year.

To create the lawnlike tabletop, cover the table with plastic; then grow rye grass in potting soil spread on top. Allow 10 to 14 days for the seeds to sprout. (For a quicker alternative, purchase sod at a local nursery.)

To attach a burlap skirt to the table, follow the step-by-step photographs at right. To estimate yardage for the burlap, measure the circumference of the table and add 18" for each pleat (see Step 2).

Step 1. Fold the top edge of the burlap under 6". Use florist's wire to attach the burlap to the mesh.

Step 2. As you attach the burlap, make a large pleat every 2 feet and wire it to the table.

Step 3. Loosely wind rope around the table. At each pleat, knot the rope into a loop and attach it to the pleat with florist's wire.

Set a small container filled with poinsettias in the center of the table. Spray pinecones, leaves, and clay pots with Floralife 24-carat gold spray paint (for a source listing, see page 156) and scatter them around the table. Place a votive candle in each pot.

Tops of the Table

Holiday happenings always seem to come together around the table. Here are five inspirational settings with looks ranging from sophisticated to sportive. Adapt your favorite to keep your table in good form throughout the season.

Above: Pull out seldom-used cups and cake plates to set a table that's old-fashioned yet polished. First, stack two pedestal-based cake stands and pile on lots of antique ornaments. Use pewter baby cups to hold tiny arrangements of ivory roses. Surround the setting with tall candlesticks.

Left: To give an arrangement of fresh fruit added richness, rub the fruit with copper and gold Rub 'n' Buff (for a source listing, see page 156). Place the fruit and some gilded leaves in a footed bowl, and trail dried grapevine among them.

Below: For a centerpiece that takes minutes to create but will last the season, plant a Christmas garden. In a large basket lined with plastic and moss, tuck pots of seasonal flowers, such as amaryllis and paperwhite narcissus, amid pots of begonias and ivy. For sculptural height, stick tall branches into the soil.

Above: Recall the bounty of Santa's sack with this easy grouping. Simply prop much-loved dolls and stuffed animals on a child's stool; nestle blocks and other favorite toys among them. To make your vignette even more irresistible, scatter red and green candy around the perimeter.

Right: Bring a garden statue and a few potted plants indoors for a fresh setting. (If you don't have a statue, consider using a large pot, small column, or basket as a focal point.) Crown the statue with a rosemary wreath and ribbon streamers. Underline the look with a vintage quilt used as a tablecloth.

733

A Door For All Seasons

Katie Stoddard, our staff photostylist, drapes her door with a lush garland of fresh greenery in winter and tropical flowers in summer.

When Katie moved to Alabama six years ago, she knew she'd have to find a use for kudzu—the astonishingly hardy, fast-growing vine that in the South is more commonplace than magnolias.

It wasn't long before Katie hit upon the idea of using dried kudzu as a framework for an overdoor garland. In the winter, she brightens the vine base with greenery and red berries; in the summer, she trains live potted vines to grow over it.

You can easily create your own all-season swag. Referring to the Diagram, screw five cup hooks into the door frame. Cut several very long lengths of dried kudzu. (If kudzu isn't abundant where you live, start with any woody vine about ¼" in diameter, wiring lengths together as needed.) Attach the vines to the cup hooks with florist's wire.

For a Christmas garland, wrap evergreen roping around the vine. Tuck in clusters of berries among the greenery, anchoring the berry stems in the vines.

In the spring, place potted flowering vines, such as clematis or trumpet vine, on either side of the doorway and train them to grow around the vine.

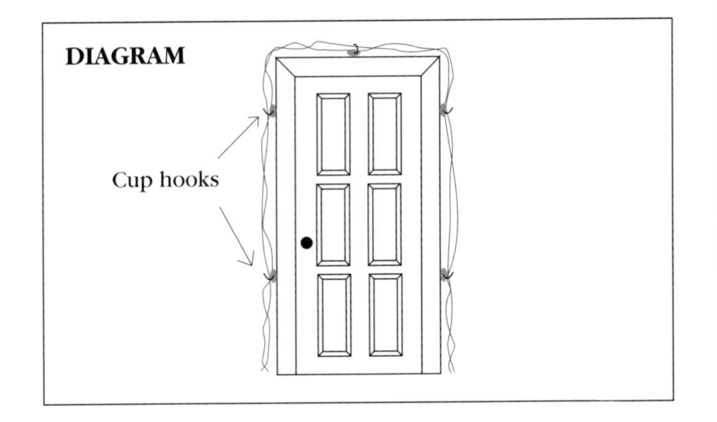

Opposite page and above: During the holidays, Katie covers her vine base with greenery, magnolia leaves, and nandina berries. In the summer, she likes to grow mandevilla—its showy pink flowers and abundant foliage completely hide the dried vines.

PUTTIN' ON THE GLITZ

The Houston decorating duo called Elfin Glitz has three R's for decorating: rediscover, rearrange, and refresh. Here's how they do it.

Though they don't sneak into houses in the middle of the night, sisters Meg Rice and Kenzie Hannah like to think of themselves as two of Santa's elves. With a bit of "elfin magic," they transform tired tinsel into holiday decorating that sparkles.

"People tend to use their stuff the same way year after year," says Meg. "Then we come in with a different perspective, and so we can create an entirely new decorating scheme, usually in one afternoon."

Meg and Kenzie are best known for what they call "memory vignettes," which they make by grouping collections with family memorabilia. "We began doing these vignettes in our own homes, using our children's keepsakes," recalls Kenzie. "Now they're popular among our clients. They're a great way to honor loved ones and remember the past while creating new traditions for the future."

Above: Clients often ask Meg Rice (left) and Kenzie Hannah (right) to create memory vignettes like this one. To contact Elfin Glitz, see the source listing on page 156.

Left: On this mantel, an evergreen swag serves as a backdrop for collections of ornaments and nutcrackers.

Right: For a dining room that glows, Meg and Kenzie lavish bright red ribbon on evergreen wreaths and garlands. Gaily wrapped presents—from the very large to the very small—become a festive centerpiece.

Above: To complement the handpainted plates designed by Texas artist Lindy Neuhaus, Meg and Kenzie fashion party favors posing as placecards. To make them yourself, wrap tulle around handfuls of candy, leaving the end of a candy cane exposed at the top of each one, and secure the bundles with matching bows. Tape name cards to the candy canes. For more information about the dishwasher-safe plates, see the source listing on page 156.

Kenzie

How to Make Your Stairway Stunning

In Meg and Kenzie's hands, plain evergreen roping becomes a magnificent holiday garland. And it's easier to make than you might think.

"This garland is really simple," says Meg, "and it's also inexpensive. We use shiny red gift wrap to almost double the thickness of the greenery. You can buy a thinner, less expensive evergreen garland and just beef it up."

To embellish the garland shown here, Meg and Kenzie use eye-catching clusters of oversized Christmas balls in red, green, and gold. But Meg adds that ribbon streamers, large jingle bells, clusters of magnolia leaves, favorite ornaments, or pinecones spray-painted gold are nice alternatives.

You will need:
evergreen garland measuring twice the length of your banister
4 yards 1"-wide green ribbon
shiny red gift wrap measuring the length of your garland (if necessary, tape sheets of gift wrap together)
florist's wire
an assortment of oversized Christmas balls
20 yards 3"-wide plaid florist's ribbon
nutcracker or other Christmas decoration
double-sided masking tape

Note: To order a fresh evergreen garland, see the source listing on page 156.

Step 1. Allowing 1 end of garland to rest on floor, tie a piece of 1"-wide ribbon around garland and handrail to secure garland to newel post. (Using ribbon instead of wire prevents damage to banister.)

Tie garland at 4 points along handrail, spacing points evenly and forming generous swags between each point.

Step 2. Cut gift wrap in half lengthwise. Starting at newel post, entwine gift wrap around garland, crumpling gift wrap in a tube-like fashion to hide plain side. Use florist's wire to secure gift wrap to garland.

Step 3. To attach clusters of ornaments to garland, cut 1 length of 3"-wide ribbon for every ornament, varying lengths as desired. Thread ribbon through top of each ornament and knot to secure.

At each of 4 points, use florist's wire to attach free ends of several ribbons to garland.

From remaining 3"-wide ribbon, tie 4 large bows and tie 1 bow to each point.

To attach nutcracker, put a piece of masking tape under its base and tape to newel post. Use florist's wire to secure nutcracker's legs to garland.

IDEAS

DECK YOUR HALLS IN MINUTES

Making your home say "Christmas" is a cinch when you play up the details. Try these tips for decorating your home in full-dress holiday finery—fast.

Above: Nestle rosy red apples and green moss in a bowl for a quick shot of seasonal color. Take your Christmas books off the shelves and set them out for friends to enjoy. Create curtain tiebacks from greenery—we used monkey's puzzle and holly—by wiring the cuttings together and fashioning the wire ends into loops to hang on window hooks.

Above: Tuck stalks of foliage, such as monkey's puzzle, nandina, and dried hydrangea, behind picture frames.

Above: For a casual snack tray, roll down the tops of lunch sacks, fill them with dried fruit and nuts, and place them in a basket.

Quick Fixes

• Ornaments aren't just for the tree. Pile them in a bowl on the coffee table, scatter them on the mantel, or tuck them in a bookcase. Wire them together in clusters to accent garlands or wreaths.

• Mix styles of candlesticks for a sideboard display. Use candles of one color to unify the arrangement. (With a little extra time, you can make your own beeswax tapers; learn how on pages 82-83.)

• It's a tradition to set out a bowl of nuts with a nutcracker. Add a colorful twist with a few sprigs of greenery and an ornament or two.

• Decorate a large mirror by suspending an evergreen or grapevine wreath with a bright red ribbon from the top of the frame.

• For a fast and elegant centerpiece, mound clove-spiked fruit in a compote. For ideas on making fruit pomanders, see pages 60-61.

• Tie ribbons on *anything*—candlesticks, baskets, serving pieces, vases, chandeliers, or chairs—to spark the pieces with holiday magic.

• Fill a tray or basket with photographs of Christmas past or cards of Christmas present.

• Follow the "golden rule" of holiday decorating with a can of spray paint. Natural materials such as leaves and seashells become festive focal points when sprayed gold and set in greenery.

• Dress up an occasional table by draping it with Christmas fabric or tapestry.

• Fill a basket or metal watering can with tall boughs of fir and holly; place it beside your front door as a welcoming gesture.

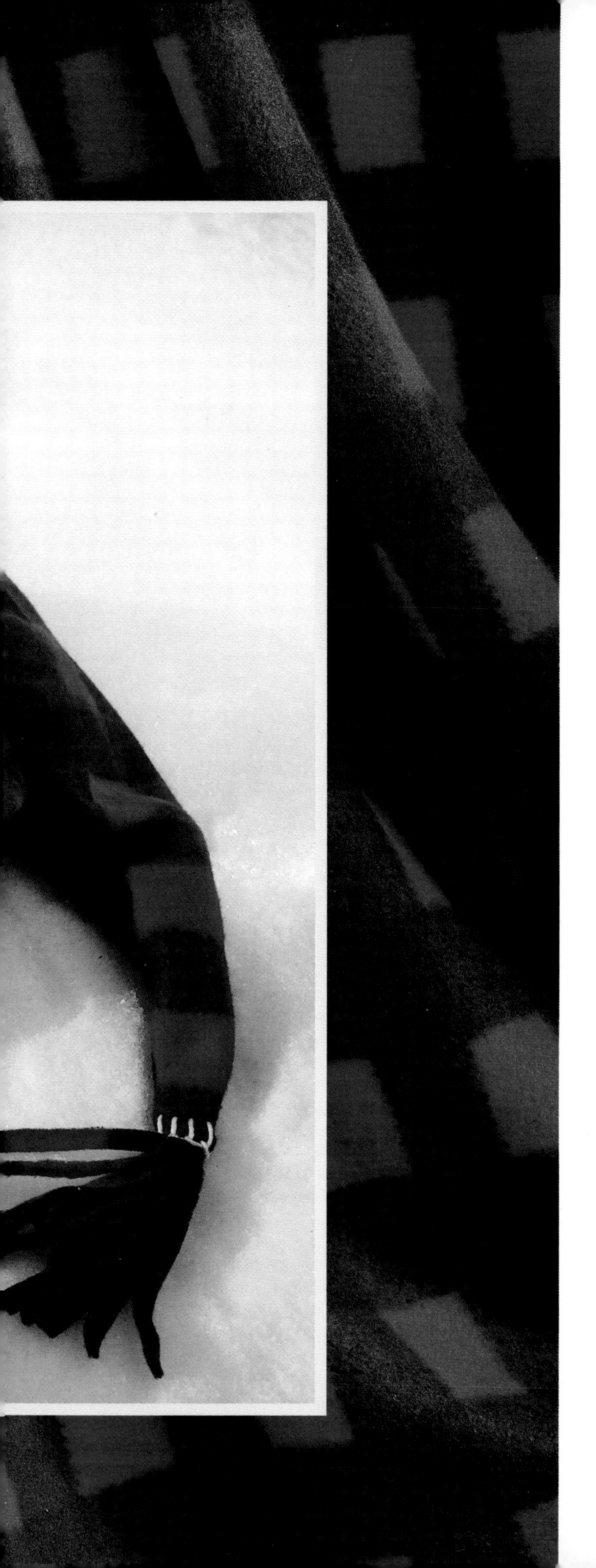

Holiday Handiwork

Let your fingers fly with our best projects for giving and keeping. Stitch bold buffalo plaid fleece into warm winter wearables. Show your style in tile with colorful mosaics. Then cover the tree with ornaments you've cross-stitched, beaded, and beribboned.

Check Mates

Winter's chill won't stand a chance against this cozy muffler and hat. Besides being warm, the polar fleece fabric is durable, machine washable, and super soft.

Muffler

Materials:
⅓ yard 60"-wide red-and-black buffalo plaid polar fleece
⅓ yard 60"-wide black polar fleece
basting thread
20 yards of white sportweight mercerized cabled cotton yarn
size 16 or 18 darning needle

Note: For fleece, see source listing on page 156.

1. From each fleece, cut 1 (10" x 60") piece. Aligning raw edges, baste pieces together, stitching 1" from edges. Trim away selvages; trim edges even.

2. Blanket-stitch through both layers around edges of muffler, hiding yarn tails between layers of fleece.

Hat

Materials:
tracing paper, pieced to make 1 (14" x 40") sheet
1⅛ yards 60"-wide red-and-black buffalo plaid polar fleece
thread to match fabric
4 yards white sportweight mercerized cabled cotton yarn
size 16 or 18 darning needle

Note: Required fabric yardage will make 2 hats. But because crosswise grain needs to go around head, it is necessary to purchase above yardage. For fleece, see source listing on page 156.

1. For head measurement, measure circumference of head, divide by 2, and add ½". Referring to Diagram 1, create hat pattern on tracing paper; cut out.

2. Cut fleece in half widthwise to make 2 (40½" x 30") pieces. Set 1 piece aside for another use. Referring to Diagram 2, with raw edges aligned, fold remaining piece in half lengthwise. Place long edge of pattern on fold and cut out, reserving excess fabric.

3. With hat still folded, stitch side seam with ½" seam allowance, tapering to ¼" seam allowance at tip of hat. Leave bottom and tip of hat open.

4. Clip seam allowance at E. Press seam open between D and E. With wrong sides facing, fold up bottom edge of hat 7". Whipstitch edge to inside of hat. Do not stitch through to outside. Turn.

5. For tassel, cut a 5" square from reserved fleece. Referring to Diagram 3, cut fringe. Fold fleece in half 3 times and handstitch across uncut edge to secure. Insert tassel into tip of hat; stitch to secure.

6. Blanket-stitch around tassel/hat seam and bottom folded edge of hat. Turn up bottom for cuff.

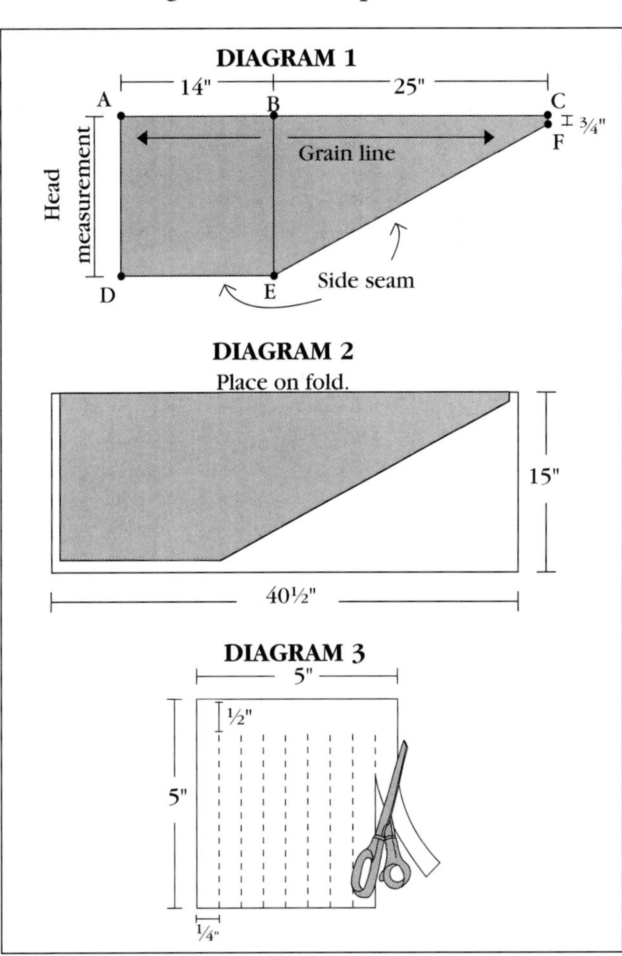

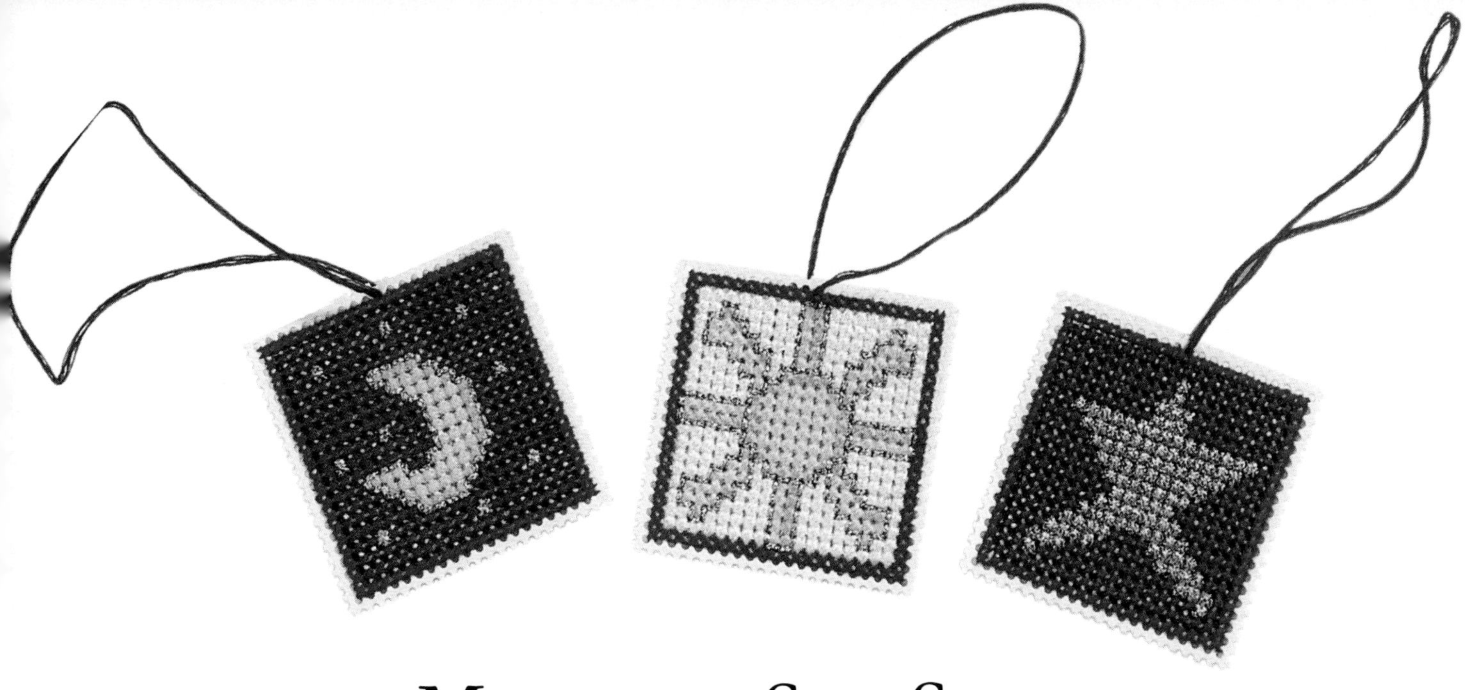

Midnight Sun Santa

Cross-stitch a celestial Santa for a pillow that glows with rich colors and gold accents. If you love the design but are short on time, stitch up a few of the border motifs for ornaments in a twinkling.

Pillow

Materials:
chart and color key on pages 140–41
16" square 14-count off-white Aida cloth
size 24 tapestry needle
embroidery floss (see color key)
½ yard fabric for pillow back
1½ yards ½"-diameter red cording
thread to match pillow back
polyester stuffing

Note: Finished design is 10" x 9¼". All seam allowances are ½". Finished pillow is 11½" x 10½". For floss and fabric, see source listings on page 156.

1. Using 2 strands of floss and stitching over 1 thread, center and work cross-stitch design on Aida according to chart. For snow, use 2 strands each of floss and blending filament.

2. With design centered, trim design piece to 12½" x 11½". From fabric, cut a 12½" x 11½" piece for pillow back.

3. Beginning and ending at bottom center of design piece, align raw edges of cording with right side of design piece. Stitch, rounding corners slightly.

4. With right sides facing, raw edges aligned, and cording sandwiched between, stitch design piece to pillow back, leaving a 5" opening at bottom edge for turning. Trim seam allowances and corners.

5. Turn pillow; stuff. Slipstitch opening closed.

Ornaments

Materials for 1 ornament:
chart and color key on page 141
2½" square 14-count white perforated paper
size 24 tapestry needle
embroidery floss (see color key)

Note: Finished design is 1½" x 1½". For floss and perforated paper, see source listings on page 156.

1. Using 2 strands of floss and stitching over 1 mesh, center and work cross-stitch design on paper according to chart.

2. Trim ornament to 1 hole outside design, being careful not to cut into any hole holding a stitch.

3. To make hanger, thread a 6" length of red or blue floss through top of ornament and knot ends together.

Paper Capers

Take a shortcut to a handcrafted look. Embellish plain purchased stationery, gift wraps, ornaments, and even lampshades with these winsome paper cutouts.

Materials for 1 cutout:
patterns on page 139
5" square of cream medium-weight paper (such as parchment or rag paper)
craft knife or small, sharp scissors
pushpin
1 tablespoon cold coffee, not instant (optional)
glue stick
item to be decorated (for sources for gift bags and boxes shown here, see page 156)
matte spray finish (optional)

1. Using pencil, transfer desired pattern to paper. Beginning at center of design and working outward, cut out white areas of pattern with craft knife. Use pushpin to make eye, nose, or other small holes.

2. If desired, place cutout in a saucer and completely cover it with coffee. Let coffee evaporate (this may take from 1 to 8 hours, depending on humidity). For a darker brown, repeat process. Let dry.

3. To mount cutout, gently and sparingly apply glue to back of cutout and press it onto surface to be decorated. If desired, apply several coats of finish, letting dry between applications.

A Menagerie of Mosaics

Mary Barnett, owner of Glass Menagerie, has learned not to cry over broken plates. In fact, she loves them—they're the basis of her fabulous mosaics. Here and on the following pages, she shows you how to make your first mosaic project a smashing success.

From bits and pieces of broken glass and ceramics, Alabama artist Mary Barnett creates beautiful mosaic accessories. On the next few pages are five projects Mary has created exclusively for the readers of *American Country Christmas*.

"Mosaic art is fun because each piece you make is unique," Mary says. "You never know what your finished piece will look like until the grout has dried."

Mary began dabbling in mosaics four years ago when she was looking for a new creative outlet. When a night class in ceramic mosaics opened up at a local studio, she jumped at the chance to learn how to make them. It wasn't long before friends and relatives were wanting to buy her creations, and in 1991 her business, Glass Menagerie, specializing in glass mosaics, was born.

You may see Mary's work in accessory shops, art galleries, and museum stores around the South. To order handmade pieces from Glass Menagerie, see the source listing on page 156. To follow her lead in making your own mosaics, keep reading.

Mary's Tips

- Making mosaics is messy work. Don old clothes, work on a well-covered surface, and always wear rubber gloves when working with the grout.
- Search flea markets, secondhand shops, and yard sales for inexpensive dishware and tiles.
- All other materials needed are available at hardware, bath, or variety stores. Bath shops often discount damaged tiles in a variety of colors.
- Buy more ceramic than you think you'll need. When you break the pieces, many fragments will be too small or irregular to use.
- Beginners should start by working on a straight-edged, flat-surfaced piece.
- Mosaics are durable, but don't leave them outside in freezing temperatures. Use them for decorative purposes only. To clean, hand-wash them and dry with a towel.

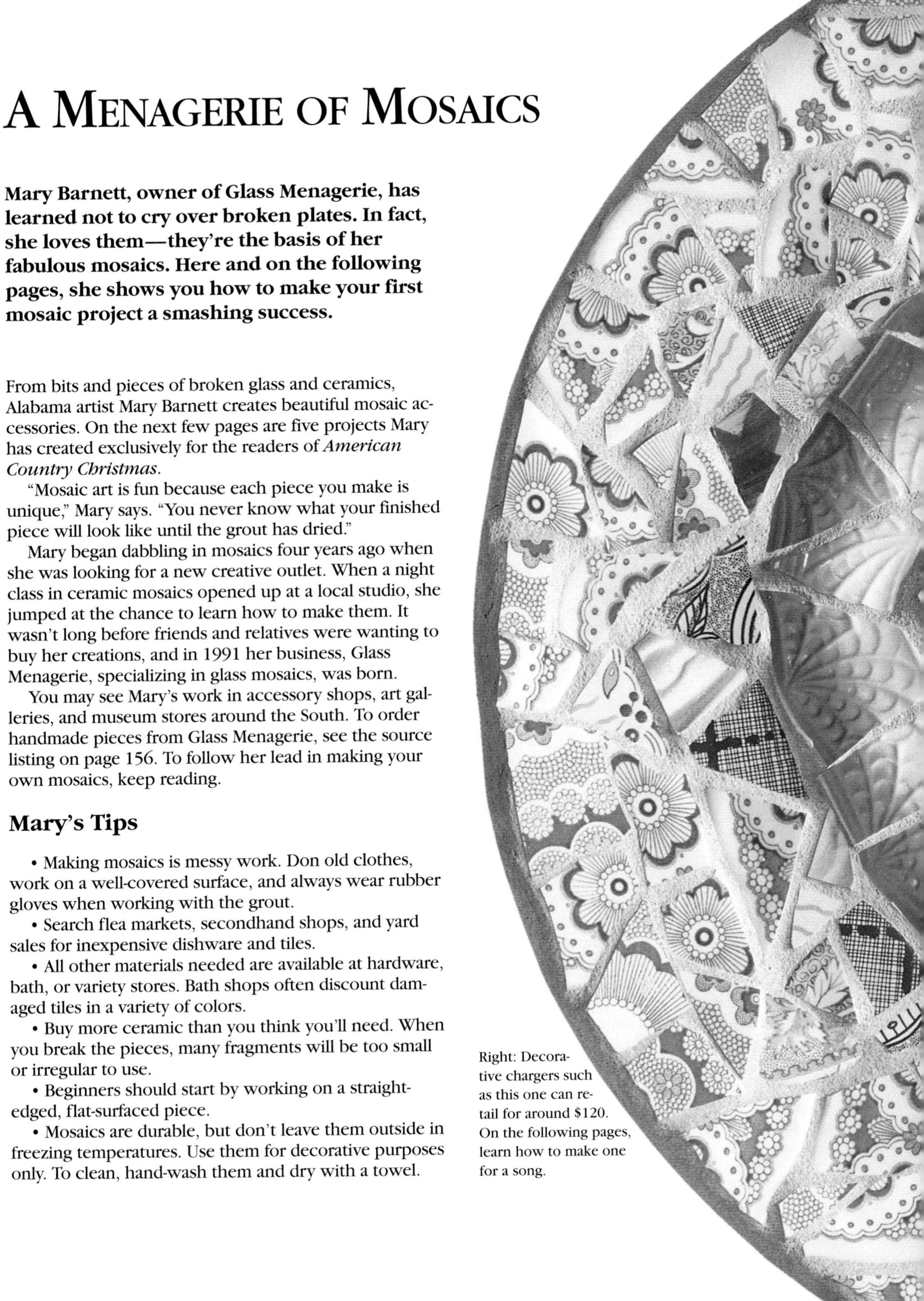

Right: Decorative chargers such as this one can retail for around $120. On the following pages, learn how to make one for a song.

Make Mosaics in Four Simple Steps

Creating handsome mosaic accessories is as easy as picking up the pieces. Here artist Mary Barnett shows you how to transform an ordinary object, like this clay planter, into a mosaic masterpiece.

You'll enjoy this project because it's practically foolproof. To ensure your safety, always wear protective goggles or glasses when breaking dishware.

You will need:
ceramic dishware or tiles
hammer
tile cutter
object to be covered (do not use plastic or paper objects)
mastic (adhesive)
masking tape (optional)
metal spatula
grout in desired color
mixing bowl and spoon
rubber gloves
sponge
silicone sealant

Step 1. To break up dishware, place dish inside a folded towel and strike with hammer. After each strike, check broken pieces for desired size.

Step 2. Arrange pieces right side up on work surface. Reshape any pieces as needed with tile cutter.

Clean and dry surface of object to be covered. Following manufacturer's instructions and working on a small area at a time, apply mastic to surface with spatula. Firmly press pieces into mastic, leaving thin spaces between them. Let dry for at least 24 hours.

Step 3. Following manufacturer's instructions, prepare grout. If desired, tape over edge of object to be left natural surface. Wearing gloves, gently smooth grout onto surface, pressing grout into spaces between pieces. Let dry for 10 minutes.

Step 4. Gently wipe surface of pieces clean with damp sponge. Let dry. Following manufacturer's instructions, apply sealant to finished mosaic piece.

Master Pieces

A child's wooden top makes a unique handle for this mosaic box. Press the handle into the mastic just as you would a piece of ceramic. The base is a hinged wooden box.

The Currier & Ives collector's plate used in the center of this platter was a flea-market find. The chip in the painted design made the collectible affordable and certainly doesn't detract from the finished mosaic. The base is a purchased ceramic charger.

IN MOSAIC

Tape off the edges of a wooden serving tray so the grout won't mar the wood. To achieve a complex design like this one, sketch it on paper first. Then experiment with arranging the pieces on your work surface before gluing them to the object.

To create the bands of alternating colors seen on this piece, draw vertical lines down the sides of the flowerpot as a guide. Tape off the top edge of the pot to leave a smooth clay lip on the finished piece. The variety of patterned dishes used makes this pot particularly charming.

Beads in Bloom

Inspired by native American designs, these flowered ornaments are a great introduction to beadwork. Finish them with chamois, an inexpensive, suede-like leather available in the automotive departments of many variety stores.

Materials for 3 ornaments:
patterns on page 150
tracing paper
wool felt scraps: dark green or dark red
chamois scraps
dressmaker's pen
1 package seed beads in assorted colors, including red, yellow, turquoise, and white
beading needle
thread to match fabrics
embroidery floss: green or red
fabric glue
3 (3/8") dark red pony beads

1. From felt, cut 6 (2¼") squares. From chamois, cut 3 (2¼") squares for ornaments and 3 (1½" x 2½") rectangles for tassels.

2. Using dressmaker's pen, transfer beading patterns to 3 felt squares as indicated on patterns.

3. Referring to Diagram 1 for stitching guide and to photograph for colors, bead ornaments as follows: Thread beading needle with thread to match felt and knot end of thread. Insert needle from wrong side of felt at beginning of 1 pattern line. Thread bead onto needle and secure by backstitching through felt and then back through bead. Continue to stitch beads as indicated. To end 1 line of beads, backstitch through last bead and knot thread on back of felt.

4. Trim each finished design piece to 1¾" square. Using 2 strands of contrasting floss, blanket-stitch around each design piece.

5. Center and glue each design piece to a chamois square. Aligning edges, glue 1 remaining felt square to back of each chamois square. Trim edges even.

6. For tassel, cut fringe on chamois tassel pieces (see Diagram 2). To form tassel, roll tightly along uncut end and glue. Stitch 1 tassel to bottom of each ornament, adding a pony bead just above tassel to hide stitching.

7. For hanger, cut 3 (¼" x 4") strips from remaining chamois. Knot ends of each strip to make a loop; glue knot to top back of each ornament.

DIAGRAM 1

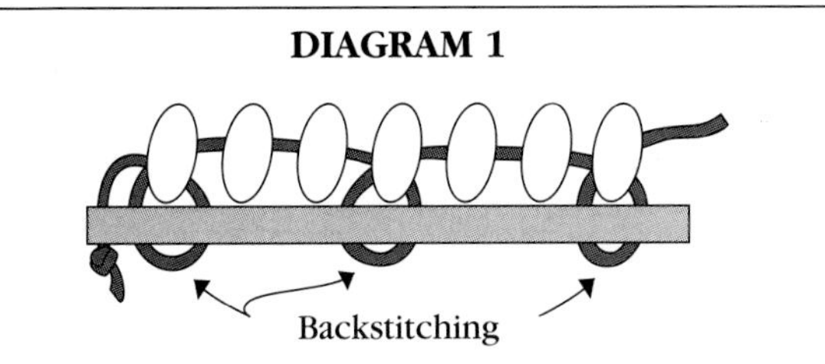

Note: When working tight curves, backstitch through all beads; when working gentle curves, backstitch through every third or fourth bead; when working straight lines, backstitch through every fifth or sixth bead.

DIAGRAM 2

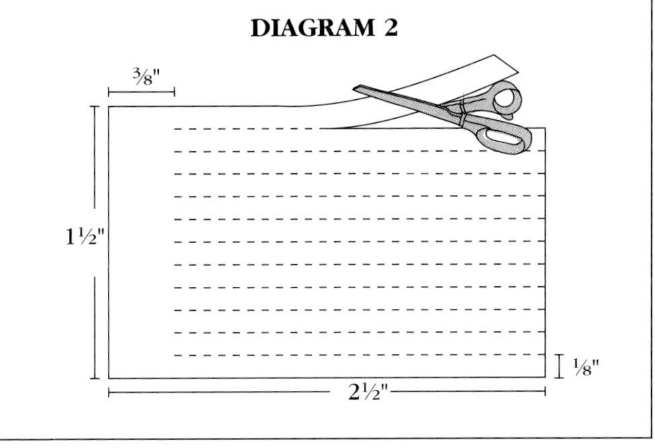

One Scrap-Happy Hobbyhorse

This old-fashioned toy is a scrap saver's dream. New Jersey designer Lou Souders recommends that you make its head from an old wool skirt, its ears from worn leather work gloves, and its body from a broomstick. The final ingredient, of course, is a child's imagination—that's when the stuffed hobbyhorse becomes a galloping bronco.

Materials:
patterns on page 142
tracing paper
$\frac{1}{3}$ yard 45"-wide herringbone wool
brown leather scrap
rust wool scrap
pinking shears
thread to match fabrics
polyester stuffing
24" length $\frac{1}{4}$"-wide black grosgrain ribbon or twill tape
2 ($\frac{1}{2}$") cream buttons
wool yarn: dark blue, green
large darning needle
36" broomstick (scraped or sanded to remove paint) or $\frac{7}{8}$"-diameter wooden dowel
4 ($\frac{3}{8}$") upholstery tacks
hammer
1 (#12) brass eye screw
52" length brown nylon cording or leather shoe string

Note: Finished size is 40" tall. Head pattern includes $\frac{1}{4}$" seam allowances. Recommended for children 3 years and older.

1. Using tracing paper, transfer patterns to fabrics and cut out. From rust wool scrap, cut 2 ($1\frac{1}{4}$"-diameter) circles for bridle rings, using pinking shears. With right sides facing and raw edges aligned, stitch head pieces together, leaving bottom edge open. Clip curves, turn, and stuff firmly to within $2\frac{1}{2}$" of bottom edge.

2. For bridle, cut the following lengths of ribbon: 10½" for cheek strap, 6" for brow strap, and 6½" for nose strap. For cheek strap, wrap ribbon around horse's head and under chin, tacking ends securely to center back seam. Attach brow and nose straps as indicated on pattern. Referring to pattern for placement, tack 1 bridle ring to each side of head.

3. Referring to pattern for placement, sew on buttons for eyes. With shiny side of leather facing, fold 1 ear piece in half and whipstitch bottom edge to head as indicated on pattern. To make ear stand up, stitch inside fold of ear to head, ⅛" above whipstitching. Repeat for other ear.

4. For mane, using darning needle, make large loops of yarn along seam from dot to dot as indicated on pattern. Make blue loops for 3", tie off blue, and then make green loops for 3". Cut loops. Knot pairs of yarn strands together along seam to secure. Fray ends of yarn.

5. Cut a 1" x 5" strip of herringbone wool. Turn long edges under ¼" and baste. Insert broomstick as far as possible into head. Stuff head firmly around stick. Wrap wool strip tightly around neck below stuffed area and secure with upholstery tacks.

6. Center eye screw on back of broomstick beneath head and screw into broomstick. Thread cording through eye screw and knot ends together for reins.

Tag Along, Little Cowboy

Round up your wildest gifts and brand them with these Western gift tags made of corrugated cardboard. (Write your message on the flat side of the tag.) The cowboy shapes double as Western-style ornaments.

Materials for 3 gift tags:
patterns on page 143
tracing paper
10" square of single-sided corrugated cardboard
red raffia
craft glue
hole punch

Note: Old packing materials are a good source for corrugated cardboard. To order new corrugated cardboard and raffia, see source listings on page 156.

1. Using tracing paper, transfer patterns to flat side of corrugated cardboard and cut out.

2. *For hat and boot:* Cut 2 (14") lengths of raffia. Referring to photographs for placement, wrap 1 length of raffia twice around each tag and knot ends; glue stars in place.

3. *For badge:* Cut 2 (3") lengths of raffia. Referring to photograph for placement, glue raffia and star to center of tag.

4. Using hole punch, punch a hole in top of each tag. Cut 3 (8") lengths of raffia. For hanger, thread 1 length of raffia through hole in each tag and knot ends.

A Tree Skirt And Stocking In the Red

Work simple stitches with embroidery floss on plain muslin and create a country classic known as redwork. The embroidered tree skirt and matching stocking will be heirloom decorations you'll display year after year.

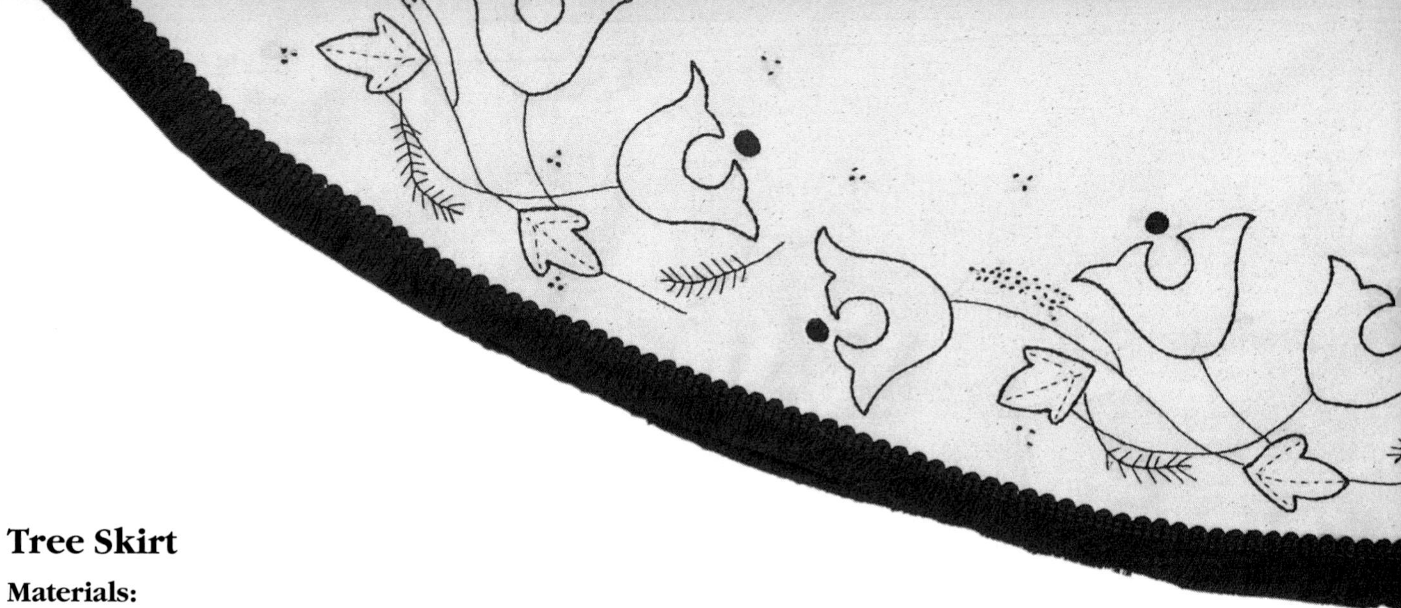

Tree Skirt

Materials:
pattern on pages 144–45
8 yards 45"-wide muslin
pushpin
1¼ yards string
dressmaker's pen
12 skeins red embroidery floss (DMC #321 shown here)
size 9 or 10 embroidery needle
6¼ yards 1"-wide red cotton fringe
thread to match fabric and fringe
2 hooks and eyes

Note: All seam allowances are ½". To set color of floss, soak skeins in solution of 1 tablespoon white vinegar and 1 cup cold water; rinse thoroughly and let dry. For floss, see source listing on page 156.

1. Cut muslin into 4 (2-yard) pieces. With selvages aligned, stitch 2 pieces of muslin together lengthwise along 1 edge. Repeat with remaining 2 muslin pieces.

2. Referring to Cutting Diagram, fold 1 muslin piece in half and then into fourths. To mark outer circle, tie pushpin to 1 end of string. Stick pushpin through folded corner of muslin. Measure 36" of string and tie loose end of string to dressmaker's pen to make a compass. Holding string taut, draw an arc with a 36" radius on muslin.

To mark inner circle, draw an arc with a 1½" radius in same manner. Cut through all layers. Open skirt; cut a straight line from outer edge to inner circle for opening. Repeat for remaining muslin piece.

3. Referring to box on page 138, transfer embroidery pattern 2" from outer edge of 1 muslin circle, repeating pattern approximately 16 times around muslin. Embroider design using 2 strands of floss. (See Embroidery Diagrams at right.)

4. With right sides facing and raw edges aligned, stitch muslin pieces together, leaving an 8" opening in straight edge of skirt opening. Clip curves and turn. Slipstitch opening closed. Press.

5. Topstitch fringe to outer edge of skirt. Stitch 1 hook and 1 eye 2" from inner circle on wrong side of skirt opening. Stitch remaining hook and eye 7" from inner circle.

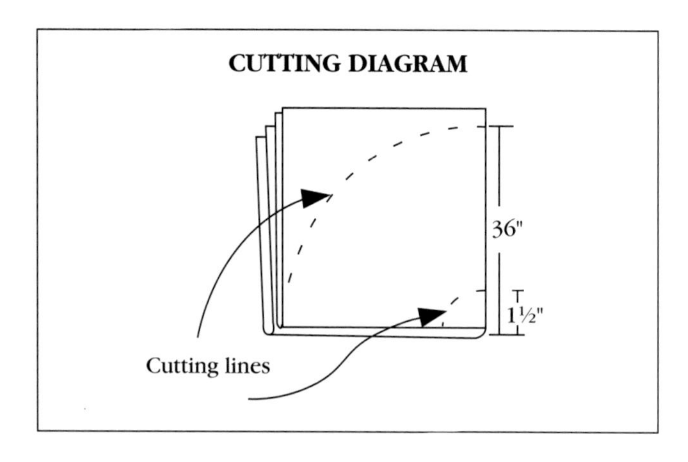

Stocking

Materials:
patterns on pages 145–46
tracing paper
dressmaker's pen
½ yard 45"-wide muslin
1 skein red embroidery floss (DMC #321 shown here)
size 9 or 10 embroidery needle
½ yard 1"-wide red cotton fringe
thread to match fabric and fringe

Note: Add ½" seam allowances to pattern. To set color of floss, soak skeins in solution of 1 tablespoon white vinegar and 1 cup cold water; rinse

thoroughly and let dry. For floss, see source listing on page 156.

1. Using tracing paper, transfer stocking pattern to muslin and cut 4. Referring to box on page 138, transfer embroidery pattern 2" from top edge of 1 stocking front. Embroider design using 2 strands of floss. (See Embroidery Diagrams below.)

2. With right sides facing and raw edges aligned, stitch embroidered stocking front to stocking back, leaving top open. Clip curves and turn. Press stocking flat.

3. To make hanger, cut a 2" x 4" piece of muslin. Turn long edges under ½"; then fold muslin in half lengthwise and topstitch both edges. Fold strip in half to make a loop. With right sides facing, raw edges aligned, and loop toward center, baste hanger to top edge of stocking back near left side seam.

4. To make lining, stitch together remaining 2 muslin pieces, leaving top edge open and 3" opening in side seam above heel. Clip curves but do not turn. With right sides facing, slip lining over stocking, matching side seams and top edges. Stitch lining to stocking around top edge, catching ends of hanger in seam. Turn stocking through opening in lining. Slipstitch opening above heel closed. Tuck lining inside stocking.

5. Topstitch fringe to top of stocking.

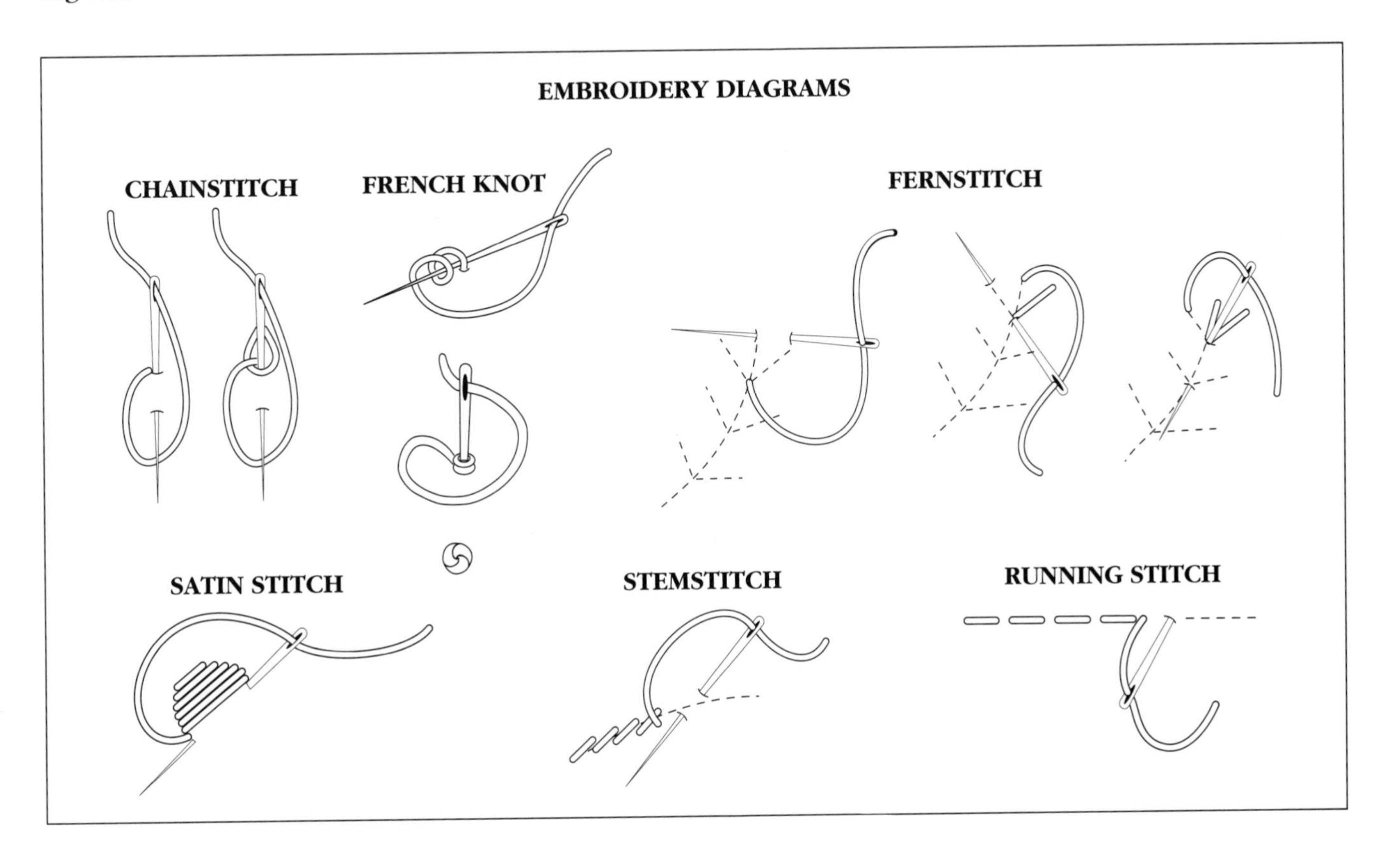

U.S. GRADE A
DUTCH GOLD
Clover
PURE HONEY
NET WT 16 OZ (1 LB) 454 g

Tweedy Bears

Paw through your remnants to gather a trio of different tweeds. Then make these movable bears for your favorite cub.

Materials for 3 bears:
patterns on pages 147–49
tracing paper
3 pieces 45"-wide brown wool tweed in varying shades: 1/4 yard for each bear
dark brown wool felt scrap
dressmaker's pen
thread to match fabrics
polyester stuffing
thin dowel (for stuffing tool)
black quilting thread
covered button forms: 4 (1 1/8") for large bear and 4 (7/8") for each small bear
long tapestry needle

Note: Patterns include 1/4" seam allowances.

1. Using tracing paper, transfer patterns to fabrics and cut out. Using dressmaker's pen, transfer all pattern markings to tweed.

2. For each bear, with right sides facing and raw edges aligned, stitch pairs of legs together, leaving open as indicated on patterns. Clip curves; turn. Repeat for body. Stuff legs and body moderately, using dowel. Slipstitch openings closed.

3. For ears, with right sides facing and raw edges aligned, stitch 1 tweed ear to 1 felt ear, leaving straight edge open. Clip curves; turn. Turn raw edge under and slipstitch closed. With felt side facing forward, fold ear slightly and stitch to head where indicated on pattern. Repeat for other ear.

4. Using black quilting thread, stitch eyes as indicated on pattern.

5. Following manufacturer's instructions, cover 4 buttons with brown tweed. To attach legs to body, using a long length of quilting thread, insert tapestry needle through body where indicated on pattern. Referring to Diagram on page 148, stitch through 1 leg and shank of 1 button. Push needle through to opposite side of body and attach opposite leg and button. Stitch back and forth several times between buttons, pulling thread tightly to indent body. Knot thread to secure. Repeat for remaining legs.

Craft a Christmas Constellation

Achieving stardom has never been easier. When you need lots of ornaments in a hurry, glue a galaxy of ribbon stars. And to custom-make a heavenly garland to suit your decor, combine an interesting roping with purchased wooden stars.

Ribbon Star Ornaments

Materials for 1 star:
pattern on page 150
heavy paper or quilter's template plastic
26" length 1"-wide ribbon or 24" length ⁷⁄₈"-wide sheer ribbon with a vertical stripe
hot-glue gun and glue sticks
10" length metallic thread
15" length gold crinkle ribbon (optional)

Note: Choose a stiff ribbon so the stars will hold their shapes. If the ribbon isn't stiff enough, starch and iron it before cutting.

1. Transfer pattern for appropriate template to heavy paper and cut out. Using template, cut 6 pieces of ribbon.

2. To form points, referring to Diagram 1, fold each piece of ribbon and glue. Referring to Diagram 2, arrange points (loop side up) and glue together at base and at top of each loop.

3. For hanger, stitch thread through 1 point and knot ends together. If desired, wrap gold crinkle ribbon around hanger and hot-glue to back of star.

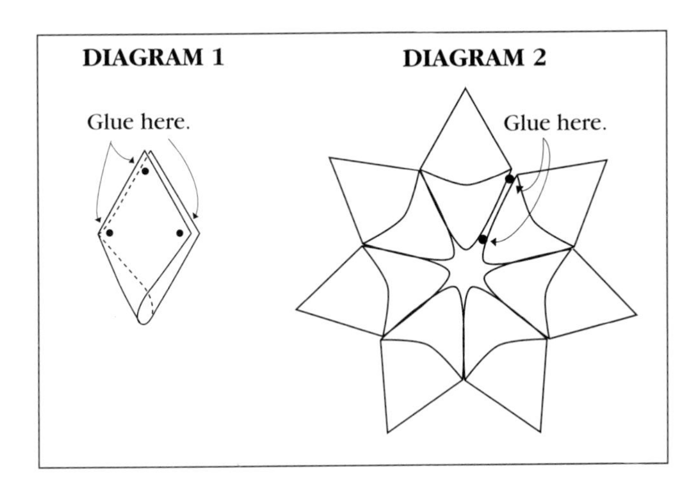

Stellar Garland

Materials for 12' garland:
25 to 35 purchased wooden stars, from 1½" to 2½" in diameter
gold spray paint
electric drill with ¹⁄₁₆" bit
string or thin ribbon
12' length ½"-diameter roping (see note below)

Note: For roping, the swag shown in the photograph above uses upholstery cording; the one on the cover uses rope. Other possibilities are braided raffia; bunched-up paper ribbon; braided or twisted yarn or macramé cording; or crinkle ribbon.

1. Spray both sides of stars with paint. Let dry.

2. Drill a hole near tip of 1 point of each star.

3. To attach stars, thread string through hole in each star and loosely tie to roping.

IDEAS

HEAVEN-SCENT

Because they look and smell divine, pomanders have long been a holiday tradition. We've given them a fresh twist by adding flourishes of tulle, gold leaf, and sumptuous ribbons.

Pomanders permeate your home with spicy fragrance. Hang them as ornaments or group them in bowls. Go ahead and make several more as gifts. (Citrus pomanders last for two to three weeks; apples stay fresh for about a month.)

Here's how to make the pomanders shown, but experiment to create your own up-to-date looks.

Making a Pomander

Begin with a clean, dry fruit. Embellish the fruit as desired, referring to the photograph for inspiration. For clove-studded fruit, use fresh, whole cloves. (Many health food stores sell cloves by the ounce, at prices well below those for grocery-store brands.) Pierce the skin of the fruit first with a pin or metal crochet hook to make inserting the cloves easier.

To hang, use florist's pins or U-shaped hairpins to attach a hanger to the top of the fruit. For heavy fruit, add a drop of hot glue to the pins.

Celestial Kumquats

For an ethereal effect, stud five kumquats with cloves and wrap each one with crinkle wire (see the source listing on page 156). Insert a short U-shaped pin into the top of each fruit; then thread all of the fruit together to form a cluster. Pin a bow to the top.

Beribboned Lemon

Encircle a lemon with fancy trimmings. Wrap lengths of ribbon around the fruit and secure with brass upholstery tacks. If desired, glue cording in a coil to the top of the fruit.

Wrapped in Tulle

Cradle a clove-studded fruit in an airy net of tulle. Push cloves into the skin of the fruit (lemon and lime are shown here, but an orange would work, too). Wrap the fruit in a 12" square of white, gold, or lime green tulle and tie it with a sheer citrus-colored ribbon. (For a source listing, see page 156.)

Clove-Studded Orange

Decorate an orange (or any other citrus) with patterns of cloves. Wrap a thin ribbon between the rows of cloves or pin it to the top or bottom.

Gilded Apple

Gild an apple for an elegant accent. Wash and dry the apple to remove all traces of wax. Following the manufacturer's instructions, apply sizing and gold leaf in randomly spaced patches around the apple. (For a complete gold-leaf kit, see the source listing on page 156.) After the gold leaf is applied, brush it with an old toothbrush to create a mottled effect. Tie sheer gold ribbon in a bow around the stem.

Pincushion instructions begin on page 64.
A source for ribbons is on page 156.

Treasured Traditions

Celebrate the best of the past with such classic creations as these fruit-shaped pincushions. We've rounded out our selection with old-fashioned crafts and recipes certain to become part of your family's holiday customs.

Fruitful Revival

Vintage fruit-shaped pincushions made from scraps of velvet are highly collectible. Our new, richly textured versions are so pretty that they're likely to bypass the sewing basket for a place on the mantel or the Christmas tree.

Materials for 3 fruit:
patterns on page 151
⅛ yard 45"-wide red rayon velvet (for apple and plum)
⅛ yard 45"-wide gold rayon velvet (for pear)
¼ cup liquid bleach
tracing paper
dressmaker's pencil
thread to match fabrics
polyester stuffing
long tapestry needle
small twig
hot-glue gun and glue sticks
1 yard 1"-wide gold metallic wire-edged ribbon
liquid ravel preventer
acrylic paints: red, purple
stencil brush

Note: Fruit patterns include ¼" seam allowances. Leaf patterns include ⅛" seam allowances.

1. To "antique" velvet, hand-wash fabric to remove sizing; rinse thoroughly. Finger-gather into small pleats along grain line. Tightly twist pleated fabric to wring out water. Set aside to dry.

For pear, combine ¼ cup bleach with 1 cup water. Lightly brush bleach mixture onto surface of wet, twisted gold fabric. As soon as color begins to change (in about 30 to 60 seconds), wash and rinse thoroughly to remove all traces of bleach. Let dry. (*Note:* Fabric dyes vary in their sensitivity to bleach; test this process on a scrap of fabric first.)

2. Iron fabric lightly from wrong side. Using tracing paper, transfer patterns to wrong side of fabric and cut out as indicated on patterns.

3. For apple and pear, with right sides facing and raw edges aligned, stitch 2 pieces together along side seams. Repeat to join remaining piece(s), matching seams at top of fruit. Clip curves, turn, and stuff firmly.

4. Turn under ¼" seam allowance at bottom edge of fruit. Using a doubled thread, run a gathering stitch around bottom edge. Pull thread tightly to close opening; secure thread.

5. For plum, repeat steps 3 and 4, matching seams at bottom of fruit. Turn under ¼" seam allowance at top edge and gather to close opening.

6. To add definition to apple, using long needle and doubled thread, sew back and forth between center top and bottom of fruit, pulling thread tightly to create indentations. Secure thread. To make cleft

on side of plum, make a row of running stitches in center of 1 panel from bottom to top of fruit. Pull threads tightly to make groove. Secure thread.

7. For stems, cut 3 (1") pieces from twig and hot-glue 1 to center top of each fruit.

8. For leaves, cut the following lengths from ribbon: 4 (3¼") for apple, 4 (3¼") for pear, and 4 (2½") for plum. For each leaf, stack 2 matching lengths together, aligning wired edges. Transfer leaf pattern to top of each ribbon stack as indicated on pattern and stitch together. Cut out leaf ⅛" from stitching line. Apply liquid ravel preventer to raw curved edge. Repeat for remaining leaves. Open leaves to right side and hot-glue 2 leaves to base of each stem.

9. To add color highlights to fruit: For apple, combine red and purple paints to make dark red. Mix 1 part paint with 1 part water to dilute. Using dry stencil brush, lightly paint fabric to achieve desired shading. Let dry. Brush surface of fruit with an old toothbrush to restore fabric nap. Repeat for plum, using more purple paint to create a darker blush. Repeat for pear, using only red paint.

APPLIQUÉ-TIONS FROM HUNGARY

Through the Sándor Collection, Leve and Carole Karvazy market pieces made by Hungarian needleworkers. Here, Leve and Carole share the secrets behind the ornaments' traditional yet simple technique: cut-felt appliqué.

Materials for teardrop or round ornament:
pattern on page 152
tracing paper
dressmaker's pen
4" square cream wool felt
4" square red wool felt
thread: red, cream
small, sharp embroidery scissors
pinking shears (for teardrop ornament)
tissue paper

Note: For source listing for wool felt, see page 156.

1. Using tracing paper, transfer desired pattern to center of cream felt.

2. Aligning edges, place cream felt (pattern side up) on red felt; pin to secure.

Fill bobbin with red thread; thread machine with cream thread and shorten stitch length. With cream side up, topstitch along dotted lines, adjusting stitch tension as needed.

3. Turn design piece red side up. Referring to photograph, carefully trim away red felt as shown, snipping just outside stitching lines. Be careful not to cut cream felt.

4. Cut out teardrop ornament along solid lines with pinking shears. Cut out round ornament along solid lines with scissors.

5. Stitch an 8" length of cream thread through top of ornament and knot ends to make hanger.

6. Cover ornament (right side up) with tissue paper and iron flat.

Left: The round and teardrop-shaped ornaments are among The Sándor Collection's most popular items. The diamond-shaped one was designed exclusively for our readers. For more on the needleworker who created the ornaments pictured here, see page 152.

Materials for diamond ornament:
pattern on page 152
tracing paper
dressmaker's pen
cream wool felt: 2 (5") squares, 1 (½" x 6") strip
5" square red wool felt
thread: red, cream
small, sharp embroidery scissors
polyester stuffing
pinking shears
tissue paper

Note: For source listing for wool felt, see page 156.

1. Using tracing paper, transfer pattern to center of 1 square of cream felt.

2. Repeat steps 2 and 3 of teardrop or round ornament.

3. Trim edges of ½" x 6" strip of cream felt with pinking shears. Fold strip in half and tack ends to wrong side of design piece at top to make hanger.

4. Cover design piece (right side up) with tissue paper and iron flat.

5. Aligning edges, stack unstitched cream square, a small amount of polyester stuffing, and design piece (right side up), with hanger extending beyond design. Fill bobbin with cream thread. Referring to photograph, topstitch squares together close to design along all edges, catching ends of hanger in seam. Trim outer edge of ornament with pinking shears.

Traditions That Travel

Leve and Carole Karvazy established The Sándor Collection in 1988 to bring crafts handmade in Leve's native Hungary to the States.

Each time the Karvazys travel to Hungary, they rediscover how rich and varied that country's folk art traditions are. The Sándor Collection's latest line features designs by Hungarian embroiderers, weavers, woodcarvers, and dollmakers, among others. For information on how to purchase items from The Sándor Collection, see page 156.

Rise and Dine: Breakfast Breads You Make Ahead

Wake up everyone in your holiday home with the aroma of freshly baked bread. And you needn't lose sleep over it, either—our directions let you prepare part or all of these recipes days, weeks, even months in advance.

Spiced Pumpkin Bread

3¼ cups all-purpose flour
1½ teaspoons baking soda
1 teaspoon baking powder
1 teaspoon ground cinnamon
¾ teaspoon ground allspice
⅔ cup butter or margarine, softened
1 cup sugar
1 cup firmly packed brown sugar
3 large eggs
2 cups canned pumpkin
¾ cup water

Combine first 5 ingredients in a large bowl; make a well in center of mixture. Set aside.

Beat butter at medium speed of an electric mixer until creamy; gradually add sugars, beating well. Add eggs, one at a time, beating after each addition. Add pumpkin and water, beating well. Add pumpkin mixture to dry ingredients, stirring just until moistened.

Spoon batter evenly into 2 greased and floured 8½- x 4½- x 3-inch loafpans. Bake at 350° for 1 hour or until a wooden pick inserted in center comes out clean. Cool in pans on wire racks 10 minutes. Remove from pans, and cool completely. Yield: 2 loaves.

Note: Bread may be frozen, in an airtight container, up to 1 month. Thaw before serving.

Apple Griddle Cakes

1 cup all-purpose flour
1½ teaspoons baking powder
½ teaspoon salt
¾ cup apple juice
1 large egg, separated
2 tablespoons butter or margarine, melted
Rich Apple Syrup

Combine first 3 ingredients in a large bowl; stir well, and set aside. Combine apple juice, egg yolk, and butter in a small bowl. Add to flour mixture, stirring with a wire whisk until blended. Beat egg white at high speed of an electric mixer until stiff peaks form; fold into batter.

For each griddle cake, pour about ¼ cup batter onto a hot, lightly greased griddle. Cook griddle cakes until tops are covered with bubbles and edges look cooked; turn and cook other side. Serve warm with Rich Apple Syrup. Yield: 8 (4-inch) griddle cakes.

Note: Griddle cakes may be frozen up to 1 month. Layer cooled griddle cakes between wax paper; place in heavy-duty, zip-top plastic bags, and freeze. To serve, remove cakes from freezer, and let thaw 15 minutes. Toast in toaster just before serving.

Rich Apple Syrup

1½ cups apple juice
3 tablespoons brown sugar
1 tablespoon cornstarch
2 tablespoons water
½ cup chopped red cooking apple
2 tablespoons butter or margarine
1½ teaspoons vanilla extract

Combine juice and sugar in a saucepan. Bring to a boil; reduce heat, and simmer 5 minutes. Combine cornstarch and water, stirring well; add to apple juice mixture. Cook over medium heat, stirring constantly, 1 minute or until slightly thickened. Stir in apple, butter, and vanilla. Yield: 1¾ cups.

Right: For an easy brunch, make and freeze Apple Griddle Cakes up to a month ahead of time. Then all you'll have left to do is make buttery Rich Apple Syrup.

Above: Try Sweet Orange Popovers instead of everyday muffins. The tender hollows are a perfect melting place for delicious Raspberry Butter.

Sweet Orange Popovers with Raspberry Butter

1 cup all-purpose flour
1 cup plus 2 tablespoons milk
2 large eggs
2 tablespoons sugar
1 tablespoon butter or margarine, melted
1 teaspoon grated orange rind
¼ teaspoon salt
Vegetable cooking spray or vegetable oil
Raspberry Butter

Combine first 7 ingredients in container of an electric blender; cover and process until smooth. Cover and chill at least 8 hours.

Grease a popover pan with cooking spray. Pour batter into pan, filling three-fourths full. Place in cold oven. Turn oven on 450°, and bake 15 minutes. Reduce heat to 350°; bake 50 to 55 minutes or until popovers are crusty and brown. Serve immediately with Raspberry Butter. Yield: 6 popovers.

Note: Popovers may be frozen, in an airtight container, up to 2 months. To serve, thaw and bake at 350° for 10 minutes or until crisp.

Raspberry Butter

½ cup butter, softened
⅓ cup raspberry preserves
¼ teaspoon grated orange rind

Beat butter at medium speed of an electric mixer until fluffy; add preserves, 1 tablespoon at a time, beating well after each addition. Add orange rind; beat well. Cover and chill. Yield: about 1 cup.

Overnight Cranberry Coffee Cake

¾ cup butter or margarine, softened
1 cup sugar
2 large eggs
2 cups all-purpose flour
1 teaspoon baking powder
1 teaspoon baking soda
1 teaspoon ground nutmeg
½ teaspoon salt
1 (8-ounce) carton sour cream
1½ cups fresh cranberries
⅓ cup sugar
1¼ cups firmly packed brown sugar
¾ cup chopped pecans
2 teaspoons ground cinnamon

Beat butter at medium speed of an electric mixer until creamy. Gradually add 1 cup sugar; beat well. Add eggs, one at a time; beat after each addition.

Combine flour and next 4 ingredients; add to butter mixture alternately with sour cream, beginning and ending with flour mixture.

Coarsely chop cranberries; press between paper towels to remove excess moisture. Combine cranberries and ⅓ cup sugar; stir well. Pour half of batter into a greased 13- x 9- x 2-inch pan. Sprinkle cranberry mixture evenly over batter.

Combine brown sugar, pecans, and cinnamon. Sprinkle half of pecan mixture evenly over cranberry mixture. Pour remaining batter over pecan mixture. Sprinkle remaining pecan mixture over batter. Cover and chill at least 8 hours. Bake, uncovered, at 350° for 35 to 40 minutes or until a wooden pick inserted in center comes out clean. Yield: 15 servings.

Giant Chocolate-Banana Muffins

¾ cup butter or margarine, softened
⅓ cup sugar
⅓ cup firmly packed brown sugar
2½ cups mashed ripe banana
3 large eggs
2 cups sifted cake flour
1½ teaspoons baking soda
½ teaspoon salt
1½ cups shreds of wheat bran cereal, crushed
1 cup chopped walnuts
1 (6-ounce) package semisweet chocolate morsels

Beat butter at medium speed of an electric mixer until creamy; gradually add sugars, beating well. Add banana; beat well. Add eggs, one at a time, beating well after each addition.

Combine flour and next 3 ingredients; add to banana mixture, stirring just until moistened. Stir in walnuts and chocolate morsels. Let batter stand 5 minutes. Spoon batter into paper-lined jumbo (3½-inch) muffin pans, filling half full. Bake at 350° for 20 to 22 minutes or until a wooden pick inserted in center comes out clean. Cool 5 minutes in pans; remove, and cool completely on wire racks. Yield: 12 muffins.

Note: Muffins may be stored, in airtight container, up to 3 days, or frozen up to 1 month.

To bake muffins in regular (2½-inch) muffin pans, grease muffin cups, and fill each three-fourths full. Bake at 350° for 18 to 20 minutes or until a wooden pick inserted in center comes out clean. Yield: 2½ dozen.

Right: You don't have to get up early on Christmas morning to serve warm Cinnamon-Raisin Angel Biscuits. You can make the dough on Christmas Eve or even earlier—the unbaked rounds can be frozen up to two months. An added advantage is the recipe's high yield—you'll have plenty of extra biscuits to give as palatable presents.

Cinnamon-Raisin Angel Biscuits

2 packages active dry yeast
½ cup warm water (105° to 115°)
5 cups all-purpose flour
1 tablespoon baking powder
1 teaspoon baking soda
¾ teaspoon salt
½ cup plus 2 tablespoons sugar
1 tablespoon plus 1 teaspoon ground cinnamon
1 cup butter-flavored shortening
1½ cups raisins
2¼ cups buttermilk
3 cups sifted powdered sugar
2 tablespoons plus 2 teaspoons milk
½ teaspoon vanilla extract

Combine yeast and warm water in a 2-cup liquid measuring cup; let stand 5 minutes. Combine flour and next 5 ingredients in a large bowl; cut in shortening with pastry blender until mixture is crumbly. Stir in raisins. Add yeast mixture and buttermilk to flour mixture, stirring with a fork just until dry ingredients are moistened. Cover and chill at least 8 hours.

Turn dough out onto a heavily floured surface. With floured hands, gently shape dough into a ball. (Do not knead dough.) Roll to ½-inch thickness; cut with a 2½-inch round cutter. Place biscuits on lightly greased baking sheets. Bake at 400° for 10 to 12 minutes or until lightly browned.

Combine powdered sugar, milk, and vanilla; stir until smooth. Drizzle glaze over warm biscuits. Yield: 32 biscuits.

Note: Biscuit dough rounds may be frozen up to 2 months. Freeze unbaked biscuits on baking sheets 2 hours or until firm. Remove biscuits from baking sheets; place in heavy-duty, zip-top plastic bags, and return to freezer. To bake, place on lightly greased baking sheets. (Let biscuits stand at room temperature while oven is preheating.) Bake at 400° for 10 to 12 minutes or until lightly browned.

Orange-Coconut Rolls

1 package active dry yeast
¼ cup sugar, divided
¼ cup warm water (105° to 115°)
½ cup sour cream
⅓ cup butter or margarine, melted and cooled
1 teaspoon salt
3½ cups all-purpose flour, divided
2 large eggs
2 tablespoons butter or margarine, melted and divided
1 cup flaked coconut
¾ cup sugar
2 tablespoons grated orange rind
Orange Glaze

Combine yeast and 1 tablespoon sugar in warm water in a 2-cup liquid measuring cup; let stand 5 minutes. Combine yeast mixture, 3 tablespoons sugar, sour cream, ⅓ cup melted butter, and salt in a large mixing bowl; beat at medium speed of an electric mixer until well blended. Add 2 cups flour; beat an additional 2 minutes. Add eggs, beating well. Stir in enough remaining flour to make a soft dough.

Turn dough out onto a heavily floured surface, and knead until smooth and elastic (about 5 minutes). Place in a well-greased bowl, turning to grease top. Cover and let rise in a warm place (85°), free from drafts, 1 hour or until doubled in bulk.

Punch dough down; turn out onto a lightly floured surface, and knead lightly 4 or 5 times. Divide dough in half. Roll 1 portion of dough into a 12- x 6-inch rectangle; brush with 1 tablespoon melted butter. Combine coconut, ¾ cup sugar, and orange rind; stir well. Sprinkle half of coconut mixture over dough. Roll up dough, starting at long side, pressing firmly to eliminate air pockets; pinch ends to seal. Cut into 1-inch slices. Place slices, cut side up, in greased muffin pans. Repeat procedure with remaining portion of dough, melted butter, and coconut mixture.

Cover with plastic wrap, and chill at least 8 hours. To bake, let dough stand 10 minutes at room temperature. Bake at 350° for 16 to 18 minutes or until golden. Remove from muffin pans, and let cool 5 minutes on wire racks. Drizzle with Orange Glaze. Serve warm. Yield: 2 dozen.

Orange Glaze

2 cups sifted powdered sugar
2 tablespoons grated orange rind
2 tablespoons orange juice
2 teaspoons vanilla extract

Combine all ingredients in a small bowl; stir well. Yield: ¾ cup.

Stuffed French Toast

½ (1-pound) package ground pork sausage
8 (1¼-inch-thick) slices French bread
5 tablespoons plus 1 teaspoon strawberry jam
1¼ cups milk
5 large eggs, beaten
2 tablespoons sugar
2 tablespoons butter or margarine, melted and divided
Commercial strawberry syrup
Garnish: fresh strawberries

Cut sausage into 8 slices; cook in a skillet until done, turning frequently. Drain and set aside.

Cut a horizontal pocket in each bread slice; spread 2 teaspoons jam in each pocket. Place 1 sausage slice in each pocket. Set aside.

Combine milk, eggs, and sugar, stirring with a wire whisk. Pour half of milk mixture into a 13- x 9- x 2-inch baking dish. Place stuffed bread slices in dish; pour remaining half of milk mixture over bread. Cover and chill at least 8 hours, turning slices once.

Preheat griddle to 350°; brush with 1 tablespoon melted butter. Place 4 stuffed bread slices on griddle. Cook 5 to 7 minutes on each side or until lightly browned. Repeat procedure with remaining butter and stuffed bread slices. Serve warm with strawberry syrup. Garnish, if desired. Yield: 8 servings.

Ham and Cheese Puffs

1 (17¼-ounce) package frozen puff pastry sheets, thawed
1 (6-ounce) package Canadian bacon
½ cup (2 ounces) shredded mild Cheddar cheese
2 tablespoons plus 2 teaspoons apricot preserves
½ teaspoon dry mustard

Unfold 1 pastry sheet, and roll into a 12½-inch square. Cut into 8 rounds with a 4-inch round cutter. Place pastry rounds 2 inches apart on lightly greased baking sheets. Place 1 slice Canadian bacon on each round. (Reserve remaining bacon slices for another use.) Top each bacon slice evenly with 1 tablespoon cheese, and set aside.

Unfold remaining sheet of pastry, and roll into a 12½-inch square. Cut into 8 rounds with a 4-inch round cutter. Combine apricot preserves and dry mustard; stir well. Spread 1 teaspoon apricot mixture over remaining 8 pastry rounds; place pastry rounds over cheese, preserves side down. Seal edges of pastry with a fork.

Bake at 375° for 15 minutes or until thoroughly heated and lightly browned. Serve warm. Yield: 8 servings.

Note: Unbaked puffs may be frozen up to 1 month. Freeze puffs on baking sheets 2 hours or until firm. Remove from baking sheets; place in heavy-duty, zip-top plastic bags, and return to freezer. To serve, place frozen puffs 2 inches apart on lightly greased baking sheets. Bake at 350° for 20 minutes or until thoroughly heated and lightly browned.

Memories
CHRISTMAS 1992

REMEMBRANCE OF CHRISTMASES PAST

This year, begin a new custom and gather your holiday keepsakes in a rustic album. By-the-numbers patterns make it easy to paint the designs. Special headings and catch-all envelope pages help you organize mementos into a pictorial history of your family, one Christmas at a time.

Materials:
patterns on page 153
1 roll kraft paper or 24 plain brown grocery sacks (with no printing)
wave-blade paper scissors
carbon paper
acrylic paints: sky blue, white, green, light green, red, yellow, dark brown, terra-cotta
small paintbrushes
black fine-point permanent marker
black felt-tipped calligraphy pen
white tempera paint
2 (12½") squares ⅜"-thick foam-core board
craft knife
craft glue
¼" hole punch
adhesive hole reinforcement circles
12½"-long stick, about 1¼" in diameter
band saw
electric drill with ¼" bit
1 yard red leather lacing

Note: To order photo corners seen in photograph and wave-blade paper scissors called for above, see source listings on page 156.

1. From kraft paper, cut 2 (15") squares for front and back covers. Using wave-blade scissors, cut 2 (12¼") squares for cover liners and 20 (12") squares (or desired number) for album pages.

2. For cover, using carbon paper, center and transfer cover design to 1 (15") square. For border, using a pencil and ruler, lightly draw a line 1¾" outside all sides of cover design. Transfer border design on top of pencil line as indicated on pattern.

For pages that will have headings, transfer border design to desired number of 12" pages, 1" from right edge (see photograph).

3. Using acrylic paints and paintbrushes, paint cover design and borders. Referring to photograph, add highlights as follows: light green to tree and holly, terra-cotta to birds and berries, and red to fox. Let dry.

4. Outline tree and animals with permanent marker. Use calligraphy pen to write desired headings on center top of each painted border page. Crumple painted cover and all pages; then smooth pages by hand.

5. To "age" painted cover, quickly and randomly wash with tempera paint and then dab paint off with a rag. Let dry.

6. To construct front cover, measure 1½" from 1 edge of 1 foam-core square and draw a line down length of square. Using craft knife, score along line to make a hinge. Place scored side down and to left and coat unscored side with glue. Center and glue painted cover right side up on foam core.

7. For back cover, center and glue remaining 15" kraft square to remaining foam-core square.

8. For front and back covers, glue excess edges to inside of covers. Center and glue a cover liner to inside of each cover. Weight covers until dry.

9. For each envelope page, glue 2 (12") album pages together along 3 sides, leaving top open.

10. On all pages, measure ½" from left and 3" from top and bottom and mark. Punch holes at marks. Back all holes with reinforcement circles.

11. Using band saw, cut stick in half lengthwise. Aligning left edges, center each stick half on top of 1 page. Mark corresponding holes. Repeat to mark holes for front and back cover. Drill holes at marks.

12. Stack pages as desired. Stack back cover (right side down), pages (right sides up), and front cover (right side up). Sandwich album between sticks and lace together with leather lacing. Tie lacing loosely on top and trim to desired length.

A Garden of Gifts

Sandy Puckett of Delaware, Ohio, creates delicate designs with pressed flowers. Here she shares her methods for this old-fashioned craft and tells you how to transform plain stationery, bookmarks, and seed packets into natural artworks.

Anything That Grows, Goes

Sandy Puckett assures us that you don't need an elaborate garden to gather enough materials for pressed-flower projects—even a windowsill herb garden will do. If you would like to start your own pressing garden, Sandy recommends pansies, violas, lobelia, and annual verbena for flowers; and ferns, ivy, thyme, rosemary, and artemesia for green foliage.

"Once you begin pressing, you'll go out in your yard and find all sorts of weeds and things that will look great in your pressed arrangements. You just have to have the eyes to see," she says. In her book and on the following pages, *Fragile Beauty: The Victorian Art of Pressed Flowers*, Sandy shares her passion and the art of pressing flowers. To order her book, see the source listing on page 156.

Pressing Matters

Cut a variety of flowers, foliage, and herbs in the morning after the dew has dried.

Press the cuttings in an old phone book: Beginning at the back, lay several cuttings of similar thicknesses on a page. Let the cuttings fall naturally into position; do not force them into shape.

Turn ¼" thickness of pages and lay more cuttings on a page. Continue until the book is full.

Place a heavy object on top of the book and let it sit for 4 to 6 weeks or until the cuttings are completely dry.

When you are ready to glue your pressed materials onto gift items, remember that the petals, stems, and tendrils are very fragile. Always use fine-point tweezers (available from hobby and medical supply stores) to handle them.

Use a thick, tacky craft glue so that the pieces will adhere to the paper quickly (Sandy likes Sobo glue). Pour some glue into a dish. Pick up the foliage with tweezers. Using your finger, dab a tiny bit of glue on the underside of the foliage and wipe off the excess. Using tweezers, position the foliage on the paper and press it gently in place.

Left: The inset photograph shows Sandy at home in her garden. For the note card in the large photograph, she formed the wreath by layering rye grass, sweet pea tendrils, and miniature thyme over a lightly penciled circle.

Above: Using fine-point tweezers to handle the foliage, dab a bit of glue on the underside of the foliage and place it on a traced circle. Once you have a thick base for the wreath, add wispy tendrils around the perimeter for interest.

Wreath Note Cards

Add thyme wreaths to purchased note cards for one-of-a-kind stationery appropriate for written invitations, quick correspondence, and thank-you notes.

Materials:
plain or embossed cream folded note cards with envelopes (about 3⅜" x 4⅞")
desired pressed foliage
fine-point tweezers
craft glue
⅛"-wide cream ribbon

1. Lightly draw a 2"-diameter circle in center of note card front. (The bottom of the glue bottle or a small paper cup are convenient patterns.)

2. Using tweezers, glue foliage to circle, layering pieces on top of each other to create a lush wreath.

3. Tie ribbon in a tiny bow and glue to bottom of wreath. Let dry.

Botanical Bookmarks

Tailor a bookmark to its recipient: Create one from ferns for the naturalist, flowers or ivy for the gardener, or culinary herbs for the chef.

Materials:
purchased bookmark (for pattern)
rice paper
fine-point tweezers
desired pressed foliage
craft glue
clear peel-and-stick vinyl shelf paper
⅛" hole punch
jute string

1. Lay bookmark on rice paper and trace outline with a pencil. Cut out ⅛" outside traced line.

2. Using tweezers, glue foliage on 1 side of rice-paper bookmark as desired; let dry. If desired, use pencil to write in names of each type of foliage.

3. Cut shelf paper slightly larger than bookmark. Remove protective covering. Press adhesive side to cover foliage and gently smooth in place.

4. Trim bookmark on traced line. Punch hole in top and loop a length of jute through hole.

Below and right: These handsome bookmarks feature snippets of common plants, such as Queen Anne's lace, moss, lavender, chives, thyme, ferns, Swedish ivy, grapevine, and sweet pea.

Above: Tiny ivy leaves and sweet pea and grapevine tendrils decorate this dainty seed packet pouch.

Seed-Packet Presents

This charming pouch is for your favorite gardener. Insert a few herbal seed packets so that the recipient can begin a pressing garden of her own.

Materials:
cream heavyweight watercolor paper
⅛" hole punch
fine-point tweezers
desired pressed foliage
craft glue
jute string

1. Using a ruler, tear paper to 5¼" x 8". Fold in half to make a 5¼" x 4" rectangle.

2. With paper still folded, lightly draw a line ½" from long open edge. Using hole punch and beginning and ending ½" from sides, punch 9 holes through both layers along line, spaced ½" apart.

3. Using tweezers, glue foliage on paper above hole-punched line as desired. Let dry.

4. Cut 2 (10") lengths of jute and knot 1 end of each length. Referring to photograph and starting at corners, lace bottom edge of pouch with jute. Tie lengths together at center. Cut a 7" length of jute and glue ends to back of pouch for handle.

COZY MITTENS FOR KNITTIN'

You'll need only a couple of hours to stitch these merry mittens, which work up quickly on big needles. Even a beginner with some previous experience can race through them—and on to the next pair.

Materials:
3½ oz. multicolor bouclé yarn (color A)
½ oz. red minimohair yarn (color B)
4 yards red worsted-weight yarn (color C for bobbles)
size 10 and 11 knitting needles
cable needle
stitch markers
stitch holders

SIZE: 4" wide and 11" long.

GAUGE: 17 sts = 4", 14/15 sts = 4" over cable pattern.

Note: Knitting Abbreviations are on opposite page. For a mail-order source for the multicolor bouclé and red minimohair yarns, see page 157.

STITCHES: Twist 5 right (T5R): Sl next 4 sts onto cable needle and hold at back of work, k 1 from left-hand needle, p 3 from cable needle, k 1 from cable needle. Make bobble (MB): K in front, in back, and in front of next st, turn and k 3, turn and k 3, turn and k 3, turn, sl 1, k 2 tog, psso (pass slipped stitch over).

RIGHT MITTEN: Using size 10 needles and 1 strand each of colors A and B held tog as 1, cast on 25 sts. Work in k 1, p 1 ribbing for 2½". Change to size 11 needles. *Row 1:* K 2, p 2, k 1, p 3, k 1, p 2, k 14. *Rows 2 and 4:* P 14, k 2, p 1, k 3, p 1, k 2, p 2. *Row 3:* K 2, p 2, work T5R on next 5 sts, p 2, k 14.

SHAPE THUMB GUSSET: *Row 1:* K 2, p 2, k 1, p 1, MB in next st using 1 strand each of colors B and C held tog as 1, rejoin 1 strand each of colors A and B, p 1, k 1, p 2, k 2, put marker on needle, k in front, in back, and in front of next st (2 st inc made), put marker on needle, k 11. *Row 2 and all even rows:* P across to last 11 sts, k 2, p 1, k 3, p 1, k 2, p 2. *Row 3:* K 2, p 2, k 1, p 3, k 1, p 2, k across to end of row. *Row 5:* K 2, p 2, T5R, p 2, k 2, inc 1 st in next st, k 1, inc 1 st in next st, k across to end of row = 5 sts between markers. *Row 7:* Rep row 3. *Row 9:* K 2, p 2, k 1, p 1, MB, p 1, k 1, p 2, k 2, inc 1 st in next st, k 3, inc 1 st in next st, k across to end of row = 7 sts between markers. *Row 11:* Rep row 3. *Row 13:* K 2, p 2, T5R, p 2, k 2, inc 1 st in next st, k 5, inc 1 st in next st, k across to end of row = 9 sts between markers. *Row 15:* Rep row 3. *Row 17:* K 2, p 2, k 1, p 1, MB, p 1, k 1, p 2, k 2, k 9 sts between markers, k across to end of row. *Row 19:* With right side facing, k 2, p 2, T5R, p 2, k 2, sl 13 sts just knitted onto a holder, k 9 sts of thumb, sl remaining 11 sts onto a second holder.

THUMB: Cast on 1 st at end of thumb sts and work even in St st on these 10 sts for 2¼" or until desired length. K 2 tog across row. Cut yarn, leaving a 15" tail. Thread tail through remaining sts and pull up tightly. Fasten off. Weave thumb seam from tip to base.

HAND: With right side facing, sl 13 sts from first holder onto size 11 needles, join 1 strand each of colors A and B. Pick up 3 sts over thumb, k 11 sts from 2nd holder onto same needle. Continue in pattern as established on 27 sts until piece measures about 4" from base of thumb, ending after a wrong side row.

SHAPE TOP: *Row 1:* With right side facing, k 2, p 2 tog, k 1, p 3, k 1, p 2 tog, k 4, k 2 tog, k 6, k 2 tog, k 2 = 23 sts. *Row 2:* P across to last 11 sts, k 2, p 1, k 3, p 1, k 2, p 2. *Row 3:* K 2, k 2 tog, p 3, k 2 tog, k 4, k 2 tog, k 4, k 2 tog, k 2 = 19 sts. *Row 4:* Work in pattern as established. *Row 5:* K 2 tog across row = 10 sts. Cut yarn, leaving a 15" tail. Thread tail through remaining sts and pull up tightly. Fasten off. Weave mitten seam.

LEFT MITTEN: Using size 10 needles, and 1 strand each of colors A and B held tog as 1, cast on 25 sts. Work in k 1, p 1 ribbing for 2½". Change to size 11 needles. *Row 1:* K 14, p 2, k 1, p 3, k 1, p 2, k 2. *Rows 2 and 4:* P 2, k 2, p 1, k 3, p 1, k 2, p 14. *Row 3:* K 14, p 2, T5R on next 5 sts, p 2, k 2.

SHAPE THUMB GUSSET: *Row 1:* K 11, put marker on needle, k in front, in back, and in front of next st (2 st inc made), put marker on needle, k 2, p 2, k 1, p 1, MB, p 1, k 1, p 2, k 2. Work in pattern as established, referring to directions for right mitten.

FINISHING: On wrong side, secure yarn ends at each bobble. Weave in yarn ends.

Further Fibers

These swatches show three stylish alternatives for your Christmas mittens. The variations use yarns readily available at knitting and craft shops.

1. Use red instead. To emphasize the classic cable design, knit the mittens in a bright red yarn and leave off the bobbles. If you select a double-knitting yarn, use 2 strands held together as 1.

2. Feature the fibers. If you knit the bobbles in the same bouclé and minimohair yarns you use for the rest of the mittens, you play up the fibers' luxurious textures and colors.

3. Herald the holidays. For mittens that celebrate the season, knit the bodies in a green yarn and the bobbles in a red one. The swatch shown here uses washable wool yarns for warmth and durability.

Knitting Abbreviations

inc—increase
k—knit
p—purl
rep—repeat
sl—slip
st(s)—stitch(es)
St st—stockinette stitch (k 1 row, p 1 row)
tog—together

IDEAS

SWEETNESS AND LIGHT

The beeswax candles sold in specialty shops are sweet-smelling, long-burning, and beautiful. They're also expensive. An economical and surprisingly easy route is to make your own beeswax tapers. Here, in four simple steps, we show you how.

Above: Hostesses will love elegant beeswax candles you've rolled yourself. Present them in an unfinished wooden cassette crate (available at crafts and music stores) tied with a shimmering bow.

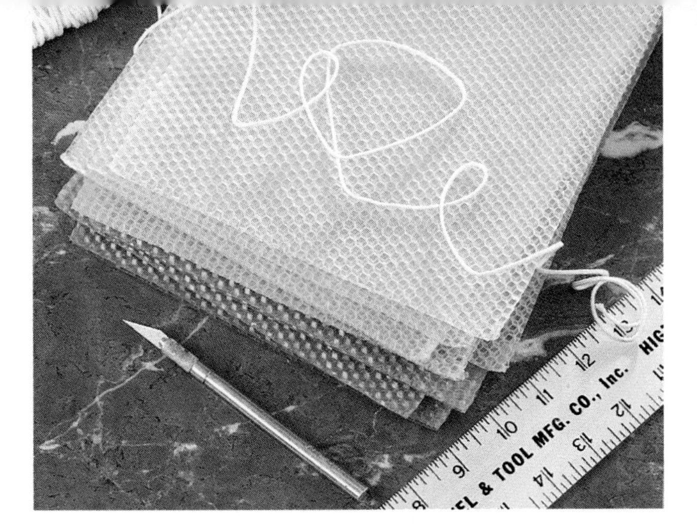

Step 1. You will need a craft knife, a metal ruler, wicking, and honeycomb-patterned beeswax sheets. To make the tapers shown here, we used #1/0 wicking and 8" x 16" sheets of beeswax (for a mail-order source, see page 157).

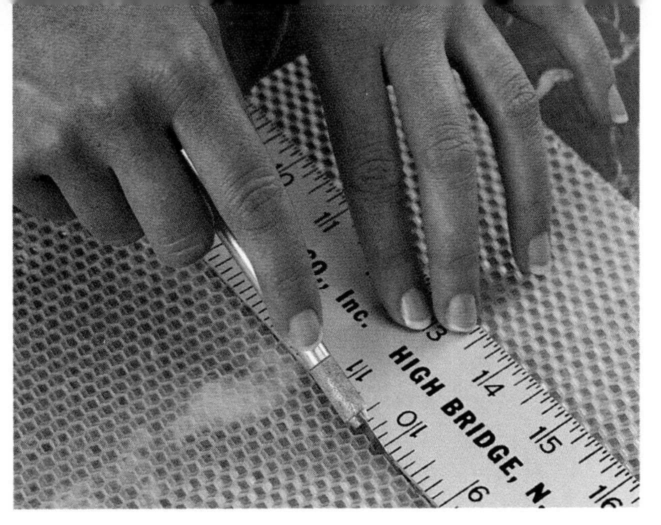

Step 2. Trim beeswax to desired size. One edge will determine taper's height; the perpendicular edge will determine its thickness. To make an 8" taper, for example, cut beeswax to measure 8" x 12".

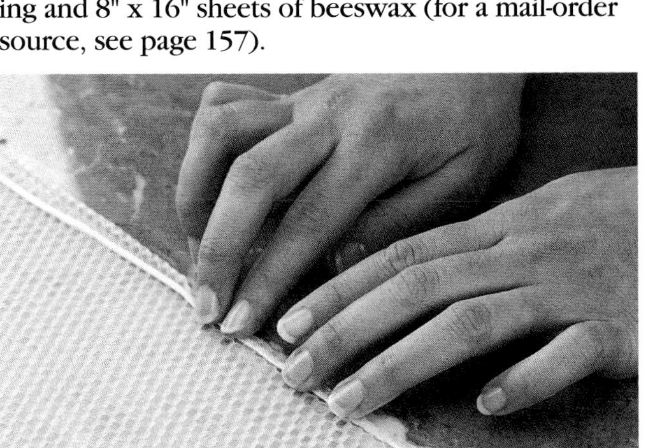

Step 3. Cut a length of wicking at least 1" longer than edge that corresponds to height. Place wick ¼" from edge, with end of wick extending beyond wax. Roll edge over wick, keeping wick taut and pressing beeswax against wick to secure.

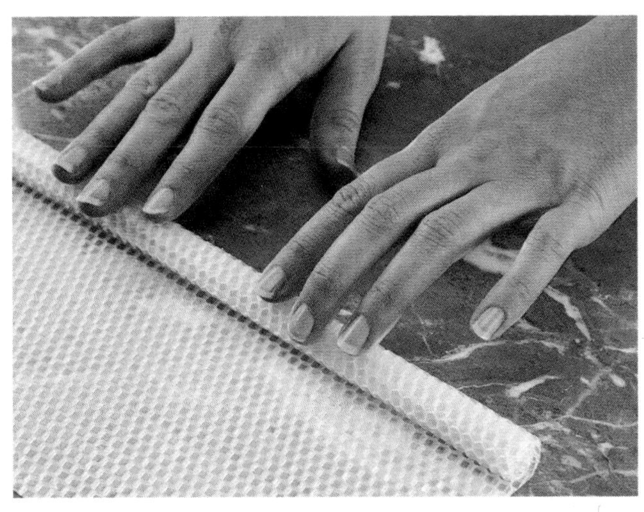

Step 4. Continue rolling evenly and fairly tightly toward opposite end. Press outside edge against candle to seal.

Taper Tips

- Because dense candles burn longer, roll the beeswax tightly. Take care, though, not to flatten the honeycomb.
- Since the wax does not need to be melted, children can make candles safely once an adult cuts the beeswax for them.
- Before rolling the candle, make sure the wick is securely pressed into the beeswax by pulling on its exposed end. If it comes out, reposition the wick and press it firmly in place.
- To make a votive, cut a long, narrow beeswax strip and roll from the short edge.
- To make spiraled tapers, cut beeswax in half diagonally, forming two triangles. Roll each triangle from the short edge to the tip.
- To create swirled tapers, stack two beeswax triangles in contrasting colors. Offset the bottom edge of the top triangle about 1" above the bottom edge of the other triangle, keeping short edges aligned. Roll the sheets together from the short edges to the tips.
- To make a thicker candle, butt the ends of two or more beeswax sheets together and roll as you would a single sheet.

Recipes for cordials and liqueurs begin on page 86.

Country Christmas Pantry

Let us help you savor the season with our favorite recipes, including these jewel-toned liqueurs blended from fruit and spices. We also serve up glorious gifts, easy parties, and projects that will trim your table in the best of taste.

Gifts Of Good Spirits

Make this European custom one of your own, and your holiday gift giving will be hassle-free. Prepare colorful cordials and liqueurs during the fall, and by Christmas all your flavorful favors will be ready.

Fresh Orange Liqueur

4 medium oranges
1 small lemon
1 cup sugar
3 cups vodka

Remove rind from oranges and lemon with vegetable peeler. Cut away any pith (white portion) from rind. Cut rind into 3-inch strips; set aside. Squeeze 1⅓ cups juice from oranges. (Reserve any remaining portions of oranges for another use.) Squeeze juice from lemon. Combine juices and sugar in a small saucepan; stir well. Cook over medium-high heat until sugar dissolves, stirring frequently. Remove from heat, and let cool. Pour mixture into a 2-quart jar. Add rind strips and vodka; stir well. Cover tightly; store in a dark place at least 2 weeks at room temperature. Shake jar gently once daily.

Pour mixture through a wire-mesh strainer, lined with cheesecloth, into glass jars; discard rind. Cover tightly. Store at room temperature. Yield: 4½ cups.

Right: Present your cordials and liqueurs in interesting bottles dressed up with fancy ribbons and bright wax seals. We gathered these bottles at recycling centers and flea markets; see page 88 for instructions on making wax seals and page 157 for a source listing for ribbons.

Fresh Orange Liqueur
Praline Liqueur
Blueberry-Spice Cordial
Raspberry Cordial
Coffee Liqueur

Praline Liqueur

2 cups firmly packed dark brown sugar
1 cup sugar
2½ cups water
4 cups pecan pieces (1 pound), lightly toasted
2 vanilla beans, split lengthwise
4 cups vodka

Combine first 3 ingredients in a medium saucepan; cook over medium-high heat until sugar dissolves. Bring to a boil; reduce heat, and simmer 5 minutes. Place pecans and vanilla beans in a 1-gallon jar. Pour hot mixture into jar; let cool. Add vodka; stir well. Cover tightly; store in a dark place at least 2 weeks at room temperature. Shake jar gently once daily.

Pour mixture through a wire-mesh strainer, lined with cheesecloth, into a bowl; discard pecans and vanilla beans. Pour mixture through a wire-mesh strainer, lined with a coffee filter, into a bowl. Change filter often. (Mixture will drip slowly.) Pour mixture into glass jars; cover tightly. Store at room temperature. Yield: 4½ cups.

Coffee Liqueur

1½ cups sugar
1 cup firmly packed dark brown sugar
2 cups water
½ cup instant coffee granules
3 cups vodka
¼ cup whole coffee beans

Combine first 3 ingredients in a medium saucepan; cook over medium-high heat until sugar dissolves. Bring to a boil; reduce heat, and simmer 5 minutes. Remove from heat, and stir in coffee granules. Let cool. Combine coffee mixture, vodka, and coffee

Cordially Yours

Make your spirited gifts memorable by showcasing them with the clever presentation seen here and on pages 84–87. Here's how.

Seal Your Bottles in Style
After decanting the liqueurs, stopper the bottles with corks (available at kitchen-supply stores).

To create the festive wax seals, melt paraffin over low heat; then melt a few crayons of the desired color in the warm paraffin. Using a paintbrush, apply wax around the cork and lip of the bottle. Invert the bottle and dip it into the wax several times, letting each coat dry.

Make Tags in Minutes
For super-fast gift tags, use a photocopier to reproduce the designs on page 155.

Serve Up Suggestions
Write serving suggestions on the back of each tag. Here are some simple ones.

• **Fresh Orange Liqueur:** Gently toss red and green seedless grapes with liqueur; cover and chill at least 30 minutes. Or drizzle liqueur over scoops of ice cream.

beans; pour into a 1-gallon jar. Cover jar tightly; store in a dark place at least 2 weeks at room temperature. Shake jar gently once daily.

Pour mixture through a wire-mesh strainer, lined with cheesecloth, into glass jars; discard coffee beans. Cover tightly. Store at room temperature. Yield: 6 cups.

Raspberry Cordial

2 (10-ounce) packages frozen raspberries in light syrup, thawed
1¾ cups sugar
¾ cup water
3½ cups brandy

Combine first 3 ingredients in a medium saucepan; stir well. Cook over medium-high heat until sugar dissolves. Bring to a boil; reduce heat, and simmer 5 minutes. Remove from heat, and let cool. Pour raspberry mixture into a 1-gallon jar. Add brandy; stir well. Cover tightly; store in a dark place at least 2 weeks at room temperature. Shake jar gently once daily.

Pour mixture through a wire-mesh strainer, lined with several layers of cheesecloth, into glass jars; discard raspberries. Cover tightly. Store at room temperature. Yield: 4¾ cups.

Honey-Pineapple Cream Liqueur

2 cups coarsely chopped fresh pineapple
½ cup sugar
½ cup water
½ cup honey
1 tablespoon lemon juice
3 cups light rum
1 (14-ounce) can sweetened condensed milk

Combine first 5 ingredients in a medium saucepan. Bring to a boil; reduce heat, and simmer 3 minutes. Remove from heat, and let cool. Pour pineapple mixture into a 2-quart jar; add rum, stirring well. Cover tightly; store in a dark place at least 2 weeks at room temperature. Shake jar gently once daily.

Pour mixture through a wire-mesh strainer into a large bowl; discard chopped pineapple. Add condensed milk; stir with a wire whisk. Pour into glass jars; cover tightly. Store in refrigerator. Yield: 5½ cups.

Blueberry-Spice Cordial

1 (16-ounce) package frozen blueberries, thawed
1½ cups sugar
½ cup water
6 whole cloves
1 (3-inch) stick cinnamon
1 whole nutmeg, cut in half
3 cups brandy

Combine first 6 ingredients in a medium saucepan; stir well. Cook over medium-high heat until sugar dissolves. Bring to a boil; reduce heat, and simmer 5 minutes. Remove from heat, and let cool. Pour blueberry mixture into a 2-quart jar. Add brandy; stir well. Cover tightly; store in a dark place at least 2 weeks at room temperature. Shake jar gently once daily.

Pour mixture through a wire-mesh strainer, lined with cheesecloth, into glass jars; discard blueberries and spices. Cover tightly. Store at room temperature. Yield: 3¾ cups.

- **Praline Liqueur:** Combine 2 cups hot coffee and ½ cup liqueur. Or combine 1 (12-ounce) jar caramel ice cream topping and 3 tablespoons liqueur; serve over baked apples, and sprinkle with crumbled shortbread cookies.
- **Coffee Liqueur:** Combine 4 cups chilled commercial eggnog and 1 cup liqueur; serve chilled. Or brush layers of chocolate cake with liqueur before frosting.
- **Blueberry-Spice Cordial:** Brush a round of Brie with cordial; sprinkle with brown sugar. Broil until sugar melts. Serve with apple wedges or gingersnaps. Or top a commercial cheesecake with blueberry pie filling mixed with a few tablespoons cordial.
- **Honey-Pineapple Cream Liqueur:** Cut ½-inch-thick slices of commercial pound cake, using a heart-shaped cookie cutter; lightly toast each cake. Brush each with liqueur and serve with fresh fruit and sweetened whipped cream. Or pour liqueur over scoops of ice cream; top with toasted nuts.
- **Raspberry Cordial:** Combine equal parts dry champagne and chilled cordial; serve immediately. Or, for a quick conserve, combine 1 (12-ounce) jar raspberry jam with 2 tablespoons cordial and ½ cup chopped toasted almonds.

BEER SALOON

Table Linens on the Double

These two looks—wild West and high country—can be yours from one basic, quick-to-make place mat.

Wild West Set

Materials:
1 yard 45"-wide natural burlap
1 red bandanna, washed and dried
16 (1½") round silver conchas (see source listing on page 157)
thread to match fabrics
water-repellent fabric protector spray
4 (10") lengths rope

1. For place mats, cut 4 (14" x 18") rectangles from burlap. For each place mat, turn each long raw edge under ¼" twice and stitch. Zigzag along each short edge, 2" from edge. To make fringe, pull out vertical threads up to zigzag stitching.

2. From bandanna, cut 16 (1" x 8") bias strips. For each place mat, measure 1½" from each corner and tack center of strip to place mat. Thread each end of strip through concha and knot on top.

3. Spray place mats with fabric protector. Hand-wash place mats in cold water; lay flat to dry.

4. For each napkin ring, tie 1 length of rope around a napkin or bandanna.

High Country Set

Materials:
1 yard 45"-wide natural burlap
½ yard 5"-wide white corded bridal lace
thread to match fabric
water-repellent fabric protector spray
4 (1") mother-of-pearl buttons
gold metallic thread
fabric glue
16 pearl seed beads

1. For place mats, repeat Step 1 for Western set. Cut 12 motifs from bridal lace. Referring to photograph, position 3 motifs on each place mat and whipstitch in place. Repeat Step 3 for Western set.

2. For each napkin ring, cut 1 (3" x 9") strip from burlap. Zigzag along 1 short edge, 1½" from end. To make fringe, pull out vertical threads up to zigzag stitching. Fold long edges under ¾" and press. Overlap fringed end 2" over unfringed end and glue. Referring to photograph, embellish 1 button with gold thread and glue 1 seed bead over each hole. Glue button to napkin ring.

Merry Christmas

Marinated Medleys

Everyone will sing your praises when you make our sweet and savory combinations. To please every palate, we created appetizers, a relish, even a dessert. And most yield large amounts, so you can keep some and package some for presents.

Zesty Cheese and Olives

10 cloves garlic, cut in half
3 cups olive oil, divided
1 cup white wine vinegar
¼ cup Dijon mustard
¼ cup lemon juice
2 tablespoons dried oregano
2 teaspoons cracked black pepper
1 teaspoon salt
1 teaspoon dried crushed red pepper
2 (7-ounce) jars Sicilian olives, drained
2 (8-ounce) packages Cheddar cheese, cut into ¾-inch cubes
2 cups kalamata olives
2 (8-ounce) packages mozzarella cheese, cut into ¾-inch cubes

Cook garlic in ½ cup oil in a medium saucepan over medium-high heat, stirring constantly, until golden. Remove from heat, and let cool. Add remaining 2½ cups oil, vinegar, and next 6 ingredients; stir well with a wire whisk.

Layer Sicilian olives and remaining ingredients evenly in 4 (1-quart) jars. Pour marinade over layers; cover tightly, and marinate in refrigerator at least 2 days. Drain before serving; serve at room temperature. Yield: 32 appetizer servings.

Note: Olive mixture may be stored in refrigerator up to 2 weeks. The longer the cheese is stored, the firmer it becomes.

Left: Zesty Cheese and Olives (left) and Lemon-Basil Vegetables (right) are easy to prepare in advance. For pretty gifts, arrange them in attractive jars; a source for these is on page 157. Singe the edges of textured paper with a match to create unique tags, and tie on herbs or flowers.

Lemon-Basil Vegetables

7 cups fresh broccoli flowerets
½ pound small fresh mushrooms
1 large sweet red pepper, cut into thin strips
1 small purple onion, thinly sliced
Rind of 1 lemon, cut into strips
1¼ cups vegetable oil
½ cup fresh lemon juice
2 teaspoons dried basil
1 teaspoon garlic salt
¼ teaspoon pepper

Combine first 5 ingredients in a large shallow container; toss gently.

Combine oil and remaining ingredients in a small bowl, stirring with a wire whisk.

Pour marinade over vegetables; toss gently to coat. Cover and marinate in refrigerator at least 8 hours, tossing occasionally. Drain before serving. Yield: 20 servings.

Note: Mixture may be stored in refrigerator up to 4 days.

Quick Antipasto

2 (6½-ounce) jars marinated artichoke hearts
1½ cups pepperoncini salad peppers, drained
1 (8-ounce) package Cheddar cheese, cut into pieces
8 ounces provolone cheese, cut into pieces
1 (7¾-ounce) can large pitted ripe olives
1 (2-ounce) jar diced pimiento, drained

Drain artichoke hearts, reserving marinade. Arrange artichoke hearts, pepper, and next 3 ingredients in rows in a shallow dish.

Combine reserved marinade and pimiento; pour over vegetables and cheese. Cover and marinate in refrigerator at least 8 hours.

To serve, transfer vegetables and cheese to a large serving platter, using a slotted spoon. Yield: 12 to 14 appetizer servings.

Note: Mixture may be stored in refrigerator up to 5 days.

Left: Quick Antipasto truly lives up to its name. To make the marinade for this mouth-watering assortment of Italian appetizers, simply add pimiento to the liquid from the marinated artichoke hearts.

Pears in Cinnamon-Berry Syrup

2 cups sugar
2 cups whole fresh strawberries, thinly sliced
2 cups water
3 (4-inch) strips orange rind
2 (3-inch) sticks cinnamon
6 large ripe pears
1¼ cups cream sherry
6 (4-inch) strips orange rind
1 (3-inch) stick cinnamon
1 vanilla bean
Orange zest

Combine first 5 ingredients in a medium saucepan; stir well. Cook over medium heat, stirring constantly, until sugar dissolves. Bring to a boil; boil 5 minutes. Remove from heat, and let cool completely. Pour mixture through a wire-mesh strainer, lined with cheesecloth, into a bowl; discard strawberry pulp, orange rind, and cinnamon sticks remaining in strainer.

Peel pears, and remove core from bottom end, leaving stems intact. Combine sherry and 1 cup strawberry syrup in a Dutch oven. Reserve remaining syrup. Bring sherry mixture to a boil. Place pears, stem end up, in pan; cover, reduce heat, and simmer 15 to 20 minutes or until pears are tender, basting often with syrup mixture. Remove from heat. Let cool.

Transfer pears and poaching liquid to a large heavy-duty, zip-top plastic bag. Pour remaining strawberry syrup over pears. Add 6 (4-inch) strips orange rind, remaining cinnamon stick, and vanilla bean; seal bag. Place bag in a large shallow dish. Marinate in refrigerator at least 8 hours, turning occasionally.

To serve, remove pears from syrup mixture. Pour syrup mixture through a wire-mesh strainer into a bowl. Reserve 1½ cups liquid; discard remaining liquid, orange rind, cinnamon stick, and vanilla bean. Place a chilled pear into each of 6 sherbet dishes. Pour ¼ cup reserved liquid evenly over each pear. Sprinkle with orange zest. Yield: 6 servings.

Note: Poached pears may be stored in refrigerator up to 5 days.

Paint Napkins with Flying Colors

With bright acrylic fabric paints and a few other items, you can give new life to plain purchased napkins.

Do the Polka

Paint a 1" border around edges of napkin. Using middle finger, finger-paint polka dots all over napkin.

Heavens Above

Paint a 1" border around napkin. Brush paint on purchased rubber stamps (see source listing on page 157) and stamp on and inside painted border.

Make Waves

Cut a length of jumbo rickrack to measure the length of 1 side of napkin. Paint 1 side of rickrack and press painted side onto edges of napkin. Paint small polka dots around rickrack imprint.

The Look of Lace

Place a manila folder over interior of napkin so that only border is exposed. Cut a small scalloped section from doily and place over edge of folder. Using stencil brush, stencil doily design onto napkin. Carefully lift doily. Continue around border of napkin.

Super Stars

Cut 1 row from a sheet of star stickers. Remove alternating stars from row; then remove entire row from backing and use as a stencil. Using stencil brush, stencil stars around edge of napkin.

Dancing Leaves

Brush paint on top of large "silk" ivy leaves (copper and gold paints are shown here). Stamp leaves all over napkin, pressing around veins on back of leaves. Allow edges of leaves to overlap.

Note: For fabric paints and the napkins used here, see the source listings on page 157.

Savory Galettes

Host a Holiday Open House

An old-fashioned open house is a great way to entertain lots of people. This menu serves 20, and our timetable, make-ahead recipes, and how-to ideas for an appetizer buffet give you everything you need for complete success. (The recipes begin on page 102.)

Cheddar-Apple Tarts

Guacamole Reds

Apricot-Cheese Truffles

Chesapeake Crab Dip

Above: Display the bill of fare, and your guests will select their appetizers with ease. Use an overhead projector pen (available at office-supply stores) to write the menu on a white plate. Later, remove the ink with window cleaner.

Below: For a fast, casual alternative to formal napkin rings, use raffia to tie sprigs of bittersweet around cloth napkins. For information about purchasing the napkins shown here, see page 157.

Timing Is Everything

Even with an informal occasion like an open house, organization is the secret to effortless entertaining. Consider these timely tips.

Four Weeks Ahead

• Set a date and time. Make out your guest list and then decide what you'll serve. Our menu serves 20, but you can halve or double it as needed.

• Consult the make-ahead notes at the end of each recipe in our menu. On your calendar, write when you'll make or assemble each dish.

Three Weeks Before

• For informal events, invitations are normally sent two weeks in advance. Since holiday schedules fill quickly, you may want to mail your invitations three weeks ahead.

• When making your invitations, consider your home's quarters—if they're cozy, stagger the times of your open house so that all your guests won't arrive at the same time.

Two Weeks to Go

• Check your supply of linens and tableware, including serving dishes of different sizes and shapes (which make a more interesting buffet table). If you come up short, ask a friend or relative to lend you a few pieces.

• Give some thought to your home's exterior. Hang wreaths, decorate your mailbox, sweep off the walkway and porch, wash front-facing windows—anything to give your place its freshest face.

Above: Lighten up with candles. For the buffet table, use votive candles (they're safer than tapers), and place them so that guests won't have to reach over them. Turn to page 157 for a source for the votive candle holders seen above.

Below: Complete the setting with a vine wreath dressed up with dried roses and bittersweet. Purchase the wreath, or see pages 110–12 to make one; hang it behind the buffet table as a festive backdrop.

Only One More Week

• Bring out the seasonal decorations. For ideas on decking your halls in minutes, see pages 32-33.

• If your open house is in the evening, make sure you have plenty of candles. For an elegant look, make your own beeswax candles—to learn how, see pages 82-83.

• Select Christmas music to play.

Countdown to Party Time

• One or two days before: Clean your house. If you're too busy, think about hiring a cleaning crew to do it for you. Or delegate specific chores to your family.

• The day before: Tidy up. Buy fresh flowers and put them in vases, or set out a few pots of paperwhite narcissus in bloom.

• Anticipate "guest geography." Arrange furniture to maximize seating, pulling into service chairs from other rooms. Place occasional or folding tables nearby.

• Set the linens and decorations on the buffet table, and plan exactly where you will place each dish. (Ideally, the buffet table should be near the kitchen so that you can serve foods quickly and easily.)

• The big day: That morning, finish preparing the food and arrange it on serving dishes. Fill additional trays so that you can replenish the buffet table by exchanging a full dish for an empty one.

• Most important of all, reserve time for a nap or a soothing bath. If you're refreshed and relaxed, you'll be able to enjoy your party every bit as much as your guests will.

Menu

Chesapeake Crab Dip
Savory Galettes
Guacamole Reds
Cheddar-Apple Tarts
Golden Onion Dip
Herbed Cashews
Apricot-Cheese Truffles
Black Forest Cheesecake Spread

Cranberry Champagne
Hot Mocha Punch

Chesapeake Crab Dip

¼ cup mayonnaise
1 (2-ounce) jar diced pimiento, drained
2 tablespoons fresh lemon juice
2 teaspoons Dijon mustard
1½ teaspoons white wine Worcestershire sauce
¼ teaspoon salt
⅛ teaspoon ground red pepper
1 pound fresh lump crabmeat, drained
⅓ cup minced celery

Combine first 7 ingredients; stir well. Combine crabmeat and celery in a large bowl. Add mayonnaise mixture; toss gently to combine. Cover and chill. Serve with French baguette slices. Yield: 3 cups.

Note: Dip may be prepared a day in advance and refrigerated in an airtight container.

Savory Galettes

1 (8-inch) round loaf sourdough bread
Cheese and Olive Spread
Pancetta Spread
3 small plum tomatoes, thinly sliced

Slice bread horizontally into 6 (½-inch) layers, using an electric or serrated knife. (Reserve any remaining bread for another use.)

Place bread rounds in a single layer on ungreased baking sheets. Broil 5½ inches from heat (with electric oven door partially opened) 4 minutes.

Spread Cheese and Olive Spread evenly on untoasted side of 3 rounds; set aside. Spread Pancetta Spread evenly on untoasted side of remaining 3 rounds. Arrange tomato slices over Pancetta Spread.

Place rounds on baking sheets, toasted side down. Broil 5½ inches from heat 3 to 5 minutes or until rounds are thoroughly heated and bubbly. Remove from oven; cool slightly.

Cut each round into 8 wedges. Arrange wedges in 6 circles on a large serving platter, alternating spreads. Serve warm. Yield: 4 dozen appetizers.

Note: Spreads may be prepared a day in advance. Refrigerate spreads in airtight containers.

Cheese and Olive Spread

1 cup (4 ounces) shredded sharp Cheddar cheese
½ cup mayonnaise
1 (4½-ounce) can sliced ripe olives, drained
3 green onions, minced
½ teaspoon curry powder

Combine all ingredients in a medium bowl, stirring until blended. Yield: about 1¾ cups.

Pancetta Spread

8 slices pancetta or bacon
¼ cup finely chopped onion
2 cloves garlic, minced
1 (3-ounce) package cream cheese, softened
3 tablespoons mayonnaise

Cook pancetta in a large skillet until crisp; remove pancetta, reserving 1 tablespoon drippings in skillet. Crumble pancetta, and set aside. Cook onion and garlic in drippings, stirring constantly, until onion is tender.

Beat cream cheese at medium speed of an electric mixer until creamy; stir in mayonnaise. Add crumbled pancetta and onion mixture; stir well. Yield: about 1 cup.

Guacamole Reds

40 cherry tomatoes
½ (3-ounce) package cream cheese, softened
1 cup mashed ripe avocado (about 1 large)
¼ cup finely chopped sweet red pepper
1½ tablespoons lemon juice
⅛ teaspoon salt
⅛ teaspoon pepper
Dash of hot sauce
¼ cup canned whole kernel corn, drained
Corn chips

Cut top off each tomato; carefully scoop out pulp. (Reserve pulp for another use.) Invert tomato shells on paper towels, and let drain 30 minutes.

Beat cream cheese at medium speed of an electric mixer until creamy. Add avocado and next 5 ingredients; stir just until blended. Stir in corn. Spoon guacamole mixture evenly into tomato shells. (Mixture may be piped into shells using a large round decorating tip.) Cover and chill thoroughly.

To serve, place layer of corn chips on serving platter; arrange Guacamole Reds on corn chips. Yield: 40 appetizers.

Note: Tomato shells may be prepared a day in advance. Refrigerate shells in zip-top plastic bags.

Cheddar-Apple Tarts

2 (9-inch) refrigerated piecrusts
4 cups unpeeled, shredded red baking apple (about 3 large)
½ cup sugar
2 tablespoons butter or margarine, melted
1 tablespoon cornstarch
1 teaspoon apple pie spice
2 teaspoons lemon juice
1 teaspoon vanilla extract
¾ cup (4 ounces) shredded mild Cheddar cheese

Roll 1 piecrust to a 14-inch circle; cut 16 rounds with a 2¾-inch round cookie cutter. Reroll remaining pieces of pastry to cut an additional 4 rounds. Fit rounds into miniature (1¾-inch) muffin pans; flute edges. Repeat with remaining piecrust. Chill 15 minutes. Bake at 375° for 5 minutes; set aside.

Combine apple and next 6 ingredients in a large bowl; toss gently to coat apple. Spoon 2 teaspoons apple filling into each tart shell. Bake at 375° for 15 to 20 minutes. Top tarts evenly with cheddar cheese. Bake an additional 5 minutes or until cheese melts. Yield: 40 tarts.

Note: Unbaked pastry shells may be frozen up to 1 month. Place pastry shells into muffin pans, and freeze 2 hours or until firm. Remove from pans, and place in heavy-duty, zip-top plastic bags. To bake, return shells to muffin pans, and thaw. Bake as directed.

Above: Toast the festive season with sparkling Cranberry Champagne chilled with Cranberry Ice Cubes (page 105). The fruit-filled ice cubes have a flavorful bonus—as they melt, they impart the tang of cranberries and pineapple juice.

Golden Onion Dip

2 large sweet onions, chopped
2 tablespoons butter or margarine, melted
½ cup chicken broth
1 (8-ounce) package cream cheese, softened
1 cup mayonnaise
½ cup coarsely chopped pistachios, toasted
Garnish: whole pistachios

Cook onion in butter in a large nonstick skillet over medium-high heat, stirring constantly, until onion is tender. Add chicken broth; bring to a boil. Cook over medium-high heat 20 to 25 minutes or until onion is golden, stirring frequently. Remove from heat, and let cool completely.

Beat cream cheese at medium speed of an electric mixer until creamy. Add mayonnaise, beating until smooth. Stir in onion mixture and chopped pistachios. Cover and chill. Garnish, if desired. Serve with assorted fresh vegetables or Melba rounds. Yield: about 3 cups.

Note: Dip may be refrigerated, in an airtight container, up to 2 days.

Herbed Cashews

1 egg white
1 teaspoon Dijon mustard
⅛ teaspoon paprika
2 cups lightly salted cashews
⅓ cup grated Parmesan cheese
1 teaspoon dried Italian seasoning
¼ teaspoon salt

Beat egg white at high speed of an electric mixer until foamy; add mustard and paprika, beating just until blended. Add cashews, stirring to coat. Combine Parmesan cheese, Italian seasoning, and salt; sprinkle over cashews, stirring well.

Spread in a single layer on a lightly greased baking sheet. Bake at 300° for 20 minutes, stirring occasionally. Cool completely on baking sheet. Store in an airtight container. Yield: 2 cups.

Note: Cashews may be frozen, in an airtight container, up to 1 month.

Apricot-Cheese Truffles

½ (8-ounce) package cream cheese, softened
2 cups (8 ounces) shredded Swiss cheese
½ cup finely chopped dried apricots
⅛ teaspoon ground white pepper
¾ cup finely chopped toasted pecans

Beat cream cheese in a large bowl at medium speed of an electric mixer until creamy; stir in Swiss cheese. Add apricot and pepper, stirring well.

Shape cheese mixture into 40 (¾-inch) balls. Roll balls in pecans, pressing firmly so pecans adhere. Serve at room temperature. Yield: 40 truffles.

Note: Truffles may be refrigerated, in an airtight container, up to 1 week or frozen up to 1 month.

Black Forest Cheesecake Spread

2 (8-ounce) packages cream cheese, softened
⅔ cup ricotta cheese
¼ cup sifted powdered sugar
½ teaspoon ground cinnamon
4 (1-ounce) squares semisweet chocolate, melted and cooled
1 cup maraschino cherries, drained and finely chopped
1 (2¼-ounce) package sliced almonds, toasted and finely chopped
6 chocolate wafer cookies, crushed
Garnishes: whipped cream, maraschino cherries, sliced almonds

Line bottom and sides of a 7-inch springform pan with heavy-duty plastic wrap; set aside.

Beat cheeses at medium speed of an electric mixer until creamy; gradually add powdered sugar and cinnamon, beating well. Slowly add melted chocolate, beating at low speed until blended. Stir in chopped cherries and chopped almonds.

Spoon chocolate mixture into prepared pan, pressing with back of large spoon to remove any air bubbles. Cover and chill at least 8 hours.

Unmold cheesecake spread onto serving plate. Dip knife in hot water; smooth surface of spread with knife. Press wafer crumbs into sides of spread. Garnish, if desired. Serve at room temperature with chocolate wafer cookies. Yield: 4 cups.

Note: Spread may be refrigerated, tightly covered, up to 4 days.

Cranberry Champagne

2 (48-ounce) bottles cranberry-raspberry drink, chilled
1 (12-ounce) can frozen pineapple juice concentrate, thawed
Cranberry Ice Cubes
2 (750-milliliter) bottles dry champagne

Combine cranberry-raspberry drink and pineapple juice in a large punch bowl; stir well. Add Cranberry Ice Cubes. Stir in champagne just before serving. Yield: 20 cups.

Cranberry Ice Cubes

2 cups pineapple juice, divided
½ cup sugar
1 (12-ounce) package fresh cranberries

Combine 1 cup pineapple juice and sugar in a medium saucepan. Bring to a boil; reduce heat, and simmer until sugar dissolves. Add cranberries. Bring to a boil over medium heat, and cook 5 minutes or just until cranberry skins begin to pop. Remove from heat, and let cool. Spoon cranberry mixture evenly into about 2½ ice cube trays. Pour remaining 1 cup pineapple juice evenly over cranberry mixture. Freeze until firm. Yield: 34 cubes.

Note: Ice cubes may be frozen up to 2 weeks.

Hot Mocha Punch

5 cups milk
4½ cups half-and-half
1 cup firmly packed brown sugar
1 teaspoon ground cinnamon
1 (12-ounce) package semisweet chocolate morsels
8 cups strong coffee
1 cup Kahlúa (optional)

Combine first 4 ingredients in a large Dutch oven; cook over medium heat until thoroughly heated. Place chocolate morsels in a medium bowl. Microwave at HIGH, uncovered, 1 minute and 30 seconds; stir until smooth. Gradually add 1 cup hot milk mixture to melted chocolate, stirring with a wire whisk until smooth. Add chocolate mixture to remaining milk mixture, stirring with a wire whisk until smooth. Stir in coffee. Add Kahlúa, if desired. Cook over medium heat until thoroughly heated. Serve warm. Yield: 20 cups.

Above: Offer your guests mugs of velvety-rich Hot Mocha Punch. Then surprise them with Black Forest Cheesecake Spread, a creamy chocolate treat you slather on chocolate wafers.

IDEAS

GUEST STARS

Company coming? Your unexpected callers will rave about these quick-fix dishes whipped up from a few simple ingredients you probably already have on hand.

Caviar Canapés

Caviar Canapés
Fill commercial canapé shells with sour cream. Sprinkle chopped fresh dill over sour cream, and top with red, yellow, or black caviar. Garnish with fresh dill, if desired.

Layered Tex-Mex Dip
Spread 2 (13-ounce) jars commercial fat-free black bean dip in a 9-inch quiche dish. Top with 1 cup commercial salsa. Cover with wax paper. Microwave at HIGH 1 minute and 30 seconds. Top with 1 cup (4 ounces) finely shredded Cheddar cheese. Microwave, uncovered, at HIGH 1 minute and 30 seconds or just until cheese melts. Sprinkle with ¼ cup sliced green onions. Serve with tortilla chips.

Dueling Salsas
Steadily and evenly pour 1 (12½-ounce) jar green salsa and 1 (12½-ounce) jar red salsa into a serving bowl at the same time. Do not stir. Serve salsas with tortilla chips.

Layered Tex-Mex Dip

Dueling Salsas

Spicy Cranberry Cheese
Combine ½ cup jellied whole-berry cranberry sauce and ½ cup jalapeño pepper jelly; stir well. Spoon mixture over 1 (8-ounce) package cream cheese. Serve with cracked pepper-topped, buttery crackers.

Spicy Cranberry Cheese

Supporting Roles

Goat Cheese Toasts
Spread softened goat cheese over French baguette slices or Melba toast rounds. Top cheese with commercial pesto and sun-dried tomato purée.

Saucy Bourbon Bites
Combine ½ cup firmly packed brown sugar, ½ cup commercial chili sauce, and ½ cup bourbon in a medium saucepan; stir well. Cook over medium heat 5 minutes. Place in a chafing dish, and serve with ham cubes.

Lemon Tortes
Cut ½-inch-thick slices of commercial pound cake with a star-shaped cookie cutter. Spread one side of each star with commercial lemon curd. Stack 3 stars together, lemon curd side up. Dollop whipped cream on top of each torte. Sprinkle with powdered sugar.

Cappuccino Sundae
Drizzle chocolate ice cream topping over scoops of coffee ice cream. Sprinkle with instant coffee granules and chocolate-coated coffee beans.

Pleasures Of the Season

Make merry with our lively lineup of crafts and foods. For openers, fashion summer flowers into winter wreaths. And for a grand finale, prepare scrumptious chocolate confections guaranteed to earn you rave reviews.

For designer Charlotte Hagood, crafting gifts and decorations from garden cuttings is the culmination of a year-long labor of love.

In the winter, she leafs through seed catalogs and daydreams about possibilities. When springtime arrives, her attention turns to planting. Summer is harvest time, and in the fall, Charlotte shapes wreaths from her garden's plenty. "Just before Christmas, it all comes together," she says with a smile.

Charlotte's method for wreath making involves three simple steps, starting with drying the harvest.

Drying Flowers and Herbs

A category of flowers called "everlastings" and many herbs are ideal, for they naturally retain their shape and color as they dry. (To see some of the plants that work well for Charlotte, turn to page 110.)

First, snip everlastings and herbs at their peak of blooming. For flowers and seedpods, strip all but the topmost leaves off the stalks. Tie the cuttings with twine into small bundles and hang them upside down in a dark, dry place for three weeks.

Weaving a Vine Wreath

"There's no big secret to making a vine wreath," says Charlotte. "All you do is make your first circle the desired diameter of your finished wreath. After that, continue adding vines until the wreath is as thick as you'd like."

You will need lengths of vines that equal at least 8 times the desired diameter of the wreath. (Supple vines such as wisteria, honeysuckle, or grapevine work nicely; you can tie shorter vines together to make longer pieces.) You will also need twine and a flat-head screwdriver.

Referring to the Diagram, tie a length of vine into a loose knot to form the wreath's diameter (Step 1).

Weave the ends of the vine around the circular base (Step 2). Cross the ends of the vine and tuck them into the wreath. You may need to use your screwdriver to wedge the ends into the wreath.

To strengthen the wreath, weave additional lengths of vine around the base (Step 3).

Adding Dried Materials

Tuck the ends of bundles of dried flowers and herbs into the vine wreath, using your screwdriver to separate the vines as needed and completely covering the vine base.

Experiment with different arrangements. For example, use only one or two plants for a monochromatic look, or select a variety for a riot of color. For a subtly ordered design, place one kind of flower at the 12, 4, and 8 o'clock positions on the wreath; place a second variety next to the first, and so on, until the wreath is full. To create a "halo" effect around the wreath, place cuttings that form long, slender spikes (such as Mexican sage or basil seed stalks) at closely spaced intervals around the outside of the wreath. For more inspiration, see the photograph on page 111.

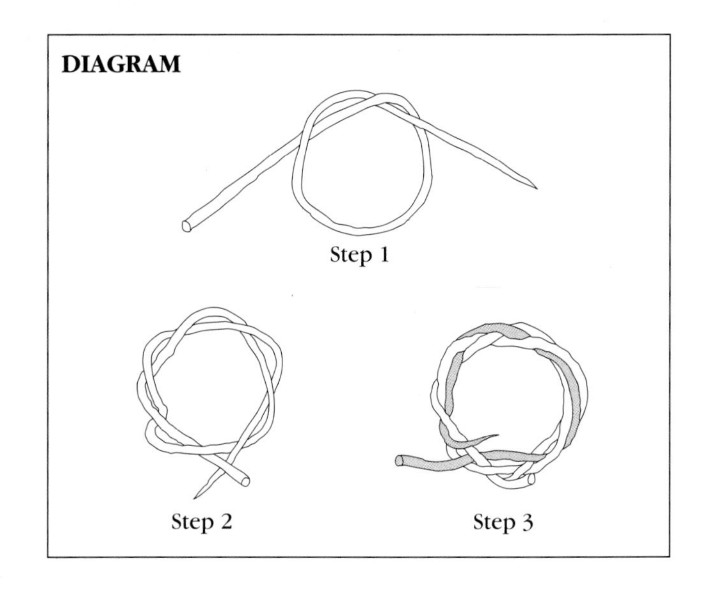

Above: Janice, Harry, and children Harry and Elle wish their friends a merry Christmas with the tangy vinegars they make.

Flavors Served Family Style

When this Texas family makes flavored vinegars for holiday gift giving, fun is the main ingredient.

Janice Schindeler has the perfect solution for making homemade gifts while involving her family in the holiday tradition—and all on a timetable that works with her busy career as food editor for the *Houston Post.*

Janice, her husband Harry Crofton, and children Harry and Elle make distinctive herb and berry vinegars year-round. So when the hectic holiday season hits, they greet it with a sideboard full of vinegars, each one fully aged, beautifully packaged, and ready for gift giving.

In the summer, Janice and the children pick blueberries and blackberries for their berry vinegars. Throughout the year, they make herb vinegars from the assortment of herbs growing in terra-cotta pots outside the back door, and they collect corks and unique bottles to showcase their beautiful blends.

"It helps keep Christmas with us all year long," Janice says. "The children stay interested because we make the vinegars a few bottles at a time, whenever the herbs and berries are available."

Young Harry and Elle help with nearly all stages of vinegar making, but their favorite job is tapping in the corks after the bottles are filled. Their dad lends a hand on the production line by sealing the corked bottles with melted wax. Janice prints the labels, listing suggested uses for each type of vinegar: hot-pepper vinegars light up steamed greens; berry vinegars add a slightly sweet tang to roast lamb or chicken; herb vinegars make great low-fat vinaigrettes for salads or marinades—just mix three parts vinegar to one part oil.

You don't have to be a food expert to prepare flavored vinegars, and if you're willing to experiment with different herbs and berries, you'll have even more fun. To learn more about making your own, along with Janice's directions on mixing kids and vinegars, just turn the page.

Making Vinegars

• Use one cupful of fresh herbs or berries or about 10 hot peppers for each pint of white vinegar.

• If you harvest the herbs from your garden, pick the leaves before the plant blooms. You can also purchase fresh herbs at a specialty grocery store or a farmer's market. In either case, wash the leaves and let them dry thoroughly.

• Put the herb leaves, berries, or peppers into glass bottles. You can purchase empty bottles at kitchen and homes stores, but it's less expensive to recycle your own. (Clear-glass wine bottles work well.)

• Add the vinegar, making sure the leaves, berries, or peppers are completely covered and there are no air bubbles.

• Cover the bottles tightly with nonmetallic caps (contact with metal spoils the vinegar). If using cork stoppers, you can seal them by dipping the neck and the cork in melted wax. (For our version of this technique, see page 88.)

• Let nature fuse the flavors. Janice says it takes 2 to 3 months for herb vinegars to age.

Kids in the Kitchen

Janice notes that her children most enjoy making vinegars when it seems spontaneous. If she sets everything up herself, Harry and Elle naturally gravitate to the kitchen and want to pitch in.

Here are more of her ideas for keeping the process fun and easy for kids.

• Don't work under a deadline. Children have individual methods and styles, and if you try to hurry them, they won't enjoy the project.

• Incorporate counting and other learning games into the activity. For example, ask a child to put 10 peppers into each jar.

• Let an adult pour the vinegar into the bottles. Even if funnels are used, this task is a bit tricky for little hands.

• Do the packaging in several stages. Cut out gift tags one night, cut ribbons on another, and tie tags and ribbons to the bottles on the third.

• When the time for gift giving arrives, let the children take the credit. They'll be proud of their creations, and you will be, too.

Above: Janice's potted herb garden includes basil, chives, dill, marjoram, oregano, and rosemary, plus garlic and hot peppers—everything needed to create a bountiful harvest of herb vinegars.

Left: For color surprise, Janice likes to use purple basil. Here she pours vinegar over the fresh herbs as Elle steadies the bottle. Next comes Elle's favorite part: tapping in the cork with a rubber mallet.

Sleepytime Plaids

Teenage girls will love these great-looking pajamas, which are quick to stitch from ready-made basics found in the men's department.

Good Night, Gown

Materials for 1 nightgown:
2 men's large plaid flannel shirts, in contrasting colors
3/4 yard 45"-wide plaid flannel, in third contrasting color
thread to match fabrics

Note: Remove all labels, collar buttons, and back loops from shirts. All seam allowances are 5/8". To prevent raveling, zigzag all raw edges.

1. Button shirts. Measure 1 1/2" below last button on each shirt and cut straight across bottom. Cut each shirt in half from top to bottom at center back.

2. Unbutton shirts. With right sides facing and raw edges aligned, stitch left half of 1 shirt to right half of contrasting shirt at center back, stitching through yoke and collar. (Save remaining halves for another use or another nightgown.) Button shirt.

3. For skirt, cut contrasting flannel in half to make 2 (13 1/2" x 45") pieces. With right sides facing and raw edges aligned, stitch short edges together to form a skirt. Run 2 rows of gathering stitches around 1 raw edge. With right sides facing and raw edges aligned, pin gathered edge of skirt to bottom edge of shirt; align side seams and gather to fit. Stitch.

4. Turn bottom raw edge under 1/2" twice and stitch hem. Fold pointed collar to inside, leaving only collar band showing. Slipstitch to secure.

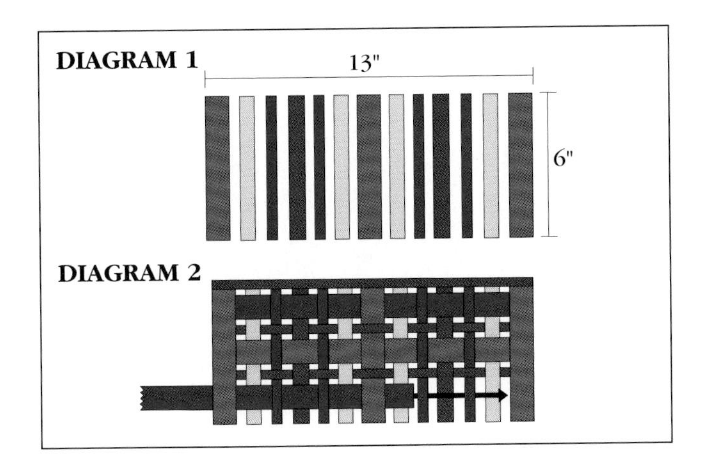

Slumber Shorts Set

Materials:
1 yard 7/8"-wide dark green grosgrain ribbon
2/3 yard 5/8"-wide yellow grosgrain ribbon
1/3 yard 5/8"-wide dark blue grosgrain ribbon
2/3 yard 3/8"-wide red grosgrain ribbon
1 1/2 yards 3/8"-wide dark blue grosgrain ribbon
3/4 yard 7/8"-wide red grosgrain ribbon
liquid ravel preventer
water-soluble marker
1 men's large white T-shirt
1/2 yard paper-backed fusible web
thread: dark blue, dark green
1 pair men's plaid flannel boxer shorts

1. For vertical stripes of design, cut the following 6" lengths of ribbon: 3 (7/8"-wide) dark green, 4 (5/8"-wide) yellow, 2 (5/8"-wide) dark blue, and 4 (3/8"-wide) red. (Reserve remaining green ribbon for use in Step 2.) Apply liquid ravel preventer to ends.

2. For horizontal stripes of design, cut the following 13" lengths of ribbon: 1 (7/8"-wide) dark green, 4 (3/8"-wide) dark blue, and 2 (7/8"-wide) red. Apply liquid ravel preventer to ends.

3. Using water-soluble marker, measure 6" down from each shoulder seam of T-shirt and mark. Using these marks as a guide, center and draw a 13"-long horizontal line across shirt.

4. Referring to Diagram 1 and aligning 1 end of ribbon with line, arrange vertical stripes, spaced 1/4" to 1/2" apart, across shirt.

5. Cut fusible web to fit 2 (13") lengths of blue ribbon. Following manufacturer's instructions, fuse web to ribbons. Peel paper backing from web and fuse ribbons horizontally across top and bottom ends of vertical ribbons. Machine-stitch along edges of horizontal blue ribbons.

6. Cut fusible web to fit remaining 13"-long ribbons. Fuse web to ribbons. Peel paper backing from web. Referring to Diagram 2 and with adhesive toward shirt, weave ribbons under and over vertical ribbons. Tuck ends of horizontal ribbons under first and last vertical ribbons. Fuse in place. Machine-stitch along edges of first and last vertical ribbons.

OUR 10 BEST CHOCOLATE GIFTS

Entice your all-time favorite chocoholics with our all-time favorite chocolate recipes. We numbered but just couldn't rank them–each sweet treat was as grand as the last.

1 Double Chocolate Cashew Tart

2 Strawberry-Chocolate Truffles

3 Chocolate-Pecan Shortbread

4 Choco-Nut Tassies

5 Mocha Fudge Walnut Brownies
6 Chocolate-Apricot Gems
7 Chocolate Chip Lemon Cake
8 Fudgy Raisin Drops
9 Chocolate Pralines
10 Scrumptious Chocolate Sauces

1 Double Chocolate Cashew Tart

For a special treat that's two gifts in one, leave the tart in the pan and wrap it with a beautiful ribbon.

1 (9-inch) refrigerated piecrust
3/4 cup semisweet chocolate morsels, melted
1 cup firmly packed brown sugar
1/2 cup butter or margarine
1/4 cup honey
3 tablespoons whipping cream
1 tablespoon vanilla extract
2 large eggs
2 cups chopped lightly salted cashews
3 (2-ounce) white chocolate-flavored baking bars
2 tablespoons whipping cream
Semisweet chocolate morsels, melted

Roll piecrust into a 12-inch circle. Place in an 11-inch tart pan with removable bottom. Trim off excess dough around edges. Spread melted chocolate over bottom of pastry, and chill.

Combine sugar, butter, and honey in a medium saucepan; stir well. Cook over medium-high heat until butter melts and sugar dissolves. Bring to a boil; reduce heat, and simmer 2 minutes, stirring occasionally.

Remove from heat; stir in 3 tablespoons whipping cream and vanilla. Cool 15 minutes.

Add eggs, 1 at a time, beating with a wire whisk after each addition. Stir in cashews. Pour cashew mixture into pastry. Bake at 350° for 20 minutes or until set. Let cool completely on a wire rack.

Combine white chocolate baking bars and 2 tablespoons whipping cream in top of a double boiler; bring water to a boil. Reduce heat to low; cook until chocolate melts, stirring frequently. Pour white chocolate mixture over cooled tart, spreading to edges of pastry.

Drop melted semisweet chocolate in small circles over white chocolate mixture in center and around edge of tart. Pull tip of a wooden pick or knife through each circle, forming small hearts.

Chill 10 minutes or until chocolate mixture is set. To serve, carefully remove sides of tart pan. Yield: 1 (11-inch) tart.

Note: Tart may be stored, tightly covered, in refrigerator up to 1 week.

2 Strawberry-Chocolate Truffles

Package truffles in inexpensive papier-mâché boxes from crafts and hobby shops.

1 (10-ounce) package frozen sweetened strawberries, thawed
3/4 cup whipping cream
4 (6-ounce) bars milk chocolate, coarsely chopped
1 1/2 teaspoons vanilla extract
1/2 cup finely chopped almonds, toasted

Place strawberries in container of an electric blender; cover and process until smooth, stopping once to scrape down sides. Pour strawberry puree into a saucepan; bring to a boil over medium-high heat. Boil 20 to 25 minutes or until reduced to 1/4 cup, stirring frequently. Stir in whipping cream; bring to a boil. Remove from heat; let cool slightly.

Place chocolate in top of a double boiler; bring water to a boil. Reduce heat to low; cook until chocolate melts, stirring constantly. Stir in strawberry mixture. Add vanilla; stir well.

Pour chocolate mixture into an ungreased 9-inch square pan lined with plastic wrap. Cover and chill at least 8 hours.

Cut chocolate mixture into 64 squares with a hot knife. Working quickly, shape each square into a ball; roll in chopped almonds. Store in refrigerator. Serve at room temperature. Yield: 64 truffles.

3 Chocolate-Pecan Shortbread

This wheel of shortbread looks even more appealing on the vintage glass plate we picked up at a tag sale. (Flea markets, secondhand shops, and restaurant-supply stores are also good sources for inexpensive china.) For a dash of color, we wove wire-edged ribbons through the open edges of the plate.

1 cup butter, softened
⅓ cup sugar
2 teaspoons vanilla extract
2½ cups all-purpose flour
½ cup finely chopped pecans, toasted
3 (1-ounce) squares semisweet chocolate, finely chopped
18 pecan halves
2 (1-ounce) squares semisweet chocolate, melted

Beat butter in a large mixing bowl at medium speed of an electric mixer until creamy; gradually add sugar, beating well. Add vanilla; beat well. Add flour, chopped pecans, and finely chopped chocolate, stirring just until blended.

Divide dough into 3 equal portions. Place 1 portion of dough on an ungreased cookie sheet; roll into a 6-inch circle. Flute edge of dough with handle of wooden spoon or fingertips. Score dough into 6 triangles. Repeat procedure with remaining 2 portions of dough.

Bake at 325° for 30 minutes. Let cool on cookie sheets 5 minutes. Remove from cookie sheets, and let cool completely on wire racks. Carefully separate disks into wedges.

Brush bottoms of pecan halves with melted chocolate; place 1 pecan half, chocolate side down, in center of each wedge. Spoon remaining melted chocolate into a small zip-top plastic bag; snip a tiny hole in 1 corner. Pipe chocolate over pecan halves. Yield: 18 shortbread wedges.

4 Choco-Nut Tassies

Wooden cassette-tape holders lined with tissue paper are versatile containers for these scrumptious tassies.

2/3 cup sugar
1/2 cup light corn syrup
2 tablespoons plus 2 teaspoons butter or margarine, melted
2 large eggs, beaten
3/4 teaspoon vanilla extract
3/4 cup finely chopped pecans
1/3 cup semisweet chocolate mini-morsels
Chocolate Cream Cheese Pastry Shells

Combine first 5 ingredients in a large bowl; stir well. Add pecans and mini-morsels; stir well.

Pour mixture into Chocolate Cream Cheese Pastry Shells. Bake at 350° for 30 minutes or until set. Cool 5 minutes in muffin pans. Remove from pans; let cool completely on wire racks. Yield: 2 dozen tassies.

Chocolate Cream Cheese Pastry Shells

1/3 cup butter or margarine, softened
1 (3-ounce) package cream cheese, softened
3/4 cup plus 1 tablespoon all-purpose flour
3 tablespoons cocoa
2 1/2 tablespoons powdered sugar

Beat butter and cream cheese at medium speed of an electric mixer until creamy.

Combine flour, cocoa, and powdered sugar; stir well. Gradually add flour mixture to butter mixture, beating well. Wrap dough in wax paper, and chill 2 hours.

Divide dough into 24 balls. Place in lightly greased miniature (1 3/4-inch) muffin pans, shaping dough to make shells. Prick bottom of each shell with a fork; cover, and chill at least 1 hour. Yield: 2 dozen (1 3/4-inch) pastry shells.

5 Mocha Fudge Walnut Brownies

For a sturdy package, fit cardboard in a zip-top plastic bag. Place the brownies inside and seal, trapping some air. Wrap in tissue paper, corrugated cardboard, and a bow.

5 (1-ounce) squares unsweetened chocolate
½ cup butter or margarine
3 large eggs
2 tablespoons light corn syrup
1 tablespoon vanilla extract
1¼ cups sugar
¾ cup plus 2 tablespoons all-purpose flour
⅛ teaspoon salt
½ cup chopped walnuts
1 tablespoon instant coffee granules
Mocha Fudge Glaze
1 ounce white chocolate, melted

Line a 9-inch square pan with aluminum foil, allowing foil to extend over edges of pan. Grease foil, and set aside.

Combine unsweetened chocolate and butter in top of a double boiler; bring water to a boil. Reduce heat to low; cook until chocolate melts. Transfer chocolate mixture to a bowl. Let cool completely. Add eggs, 1 at a time, beating at medium-low speed of an electric mixer after each addition just until blended. Stir in corn syrup and vanilla.

Combine sugar and next 4 ingredients; add to chocolate mixture, stirring just until blended. Pour batter into prepared pan. Bake at 325° for 25 minutes. (Brownies will not test done.) Let cool completely in pan on a wire rack.

Spoon Mocha Fudge Glaze over brownies, spreading with a rubber spatula to smooth surface. Spoon melted white chocolate into a zip-top plastic bag; snip a tiny hole in 1 corner. Pipe chocolate in parallel lines, ½ inch apart, across brownies. Pull the point of a wooden pick through white chocolate lines perpendicular to the lines to create pattern. Chill 15 minutes or until glaze is set. Cover; let stand at least 8 hours at room temperature. Uncover and lift foil out of pan. Cut into bars. Yield: 20 brownies.

Mocha Fudge Glaze

⅓ cup whipping cream
1 teaspoon instant coffee granules
3 (1-ounce) squares semisweet chocolate, coarsely chopped

Combine whipping cream and coffee in a saucepan; bring to a boil over medium heat. Remove from heat; stir until coffee dissolves. Place chocolate in a bowl; pour hot coffee mixture over chocolate. Let stand 5 minutes; stir until smooth. Let stand 15 minutes or until spreadable. Yield: about ½ cup.

6 Chocolate-Apricot Gems

Showcase these diamond-shaped delicacies in wooden crates lined with handmade tissue paper and tied with sheer ribbon.

1 (6-ounce) package dried apricots, coarsely chopped
3 tablespoons sugar
⅓ cup water
1 cup butter
1 cup firmly packed brown sugar
⅓ cup sugar
3 (6-ounce) packages semisweet chocolate morsels
½ (4-ounce) bar bittersweet chocolate, chopped
5 large eggs
1 tablespoon vanilla extract
1½ cups all-purpose flour
¼ teaspoon salt
2 ounces white chocolate, melted

Line a 13- x 9- x 2-inch pan with aluminum foil, allowing foil to extend over narrow ends of pan. Grease foil, and set aside.

Combine first 3 ingredients in a saucepan; cook over medium heat until water is absorbed, stirring frequently.

Position knife blade in food processor bowl; add apricot mixture. Process 30 seconds or until almost smooth. Transfer mixture to a bowl; set aside, and let cool completely.

Melt butter in a saucepan; add sugars. Cook over medium heat until sugars melt, stirring frequently.

Position knife blade in food processor bowl; add semisweet and bittersweet chocolates. Process 1 minute or until chocolate is finely chopped. Remove food pusher. Slowly pour hot sugar mixture through food chute with processor running, blending until chocolate melts. Add eggs and vanilla; process 10 seconds.

Combine flour and salt; add to chocolate mixture. Process 30 seconds or just until blended, scraping sides of processor bowl once. Add apricot mixture; pulse 5 or 6 times or just until blended. Spread batter evenly into prepared pan. Bake at 350° for 30 minutes. (Do not overbake.) Let cool completely in pan on a wire rack. Cover and freeze at least 8 hours.

Carefully lift foil out of pan; invert frozen mixture onto cutting board. Remove foil, leaving smooth side up. Let stand 15 minutes. Cut into 1-inch diamond shapes, using a sharp knife. Spoon melted white chocolate into a zip-top bag; snip a tiny hole in 1 corner of bag. Pipe chocolate in a zigzag design over diamond shapes. Store in refrigerator. Yield: 6½ dozen.

Note: Baked chocolate mixture may be frozen, tightly covered, up to 2 weeks before cutting.

7 Chocolate Chip Lemon Cake

Present this supermoist cake, garnished with lemon rind curls, on a serving plate.

½ cup butter or margarine, softened
1 cup sugar, divided
2 large eggs
1⅔ cups all-purpose flour
1 teaspoon baking powder
½ teaspoon baking soda
½ teaspoon salt
½ cup ground toasted almonds
1 teaspoon grated lemon rind
1 (8-ounce) carton sour cream
¾ cup semisweet chocolate mini-morsels
1 teaspoon vanilla extract
¼ teaspoon lemon extract
3 tablespoons frozen lemonade concentrate, thawed
2 tablespoons water
Chocolate Glaze

Beat butter at medium speed of an electric mixer until creamy. Gradually add ⅔ cup sugar; beat well. Add eggs, 1 at a time, beating after each addition.

Combine flour and next 5 ingredients; add to butter mixture alternately with sour cream, beginning and ending with flour mixture. Mix after each addition. Stir in mini-morsels and flavorings. Pour batter into a greased and floured 6-cup Bundt pan. Bake at 350° for 35 to 40 minutes or until a wooden pick inserted in center comes out clean.

Combine remaining ⅓ cup sugar, lemonade concentrate, and water in a saucepan. Bring to a boil; reduce heat, and simmer 1 minute. Pour lemon syrup over cake in pan; let stand 10 minutes. Remove cake from pan; let cool on a wire rack. Drizzle Chocolate Glaze over cake. Yield: 1 (7½-inch) cake.

Chocolate Glaze

1 cup sifted powdered sugar
1½ tablespoons cocoa
2 tablespoons hot water
1½ tablespoons butter or margarine, melted

Combine powdered sugar and cocoa; set aside. Combine hot water and butter; stir well. Add butter mixture to sugar mixture; stir well. Yield: ½ cup.

8 Fudgy Raisin Drops

Roll a stack of these chocolaty cookies in plastic wrap; then wrap with tissue paper, corrugated cardboard, and bright ribbon.

7 (1-ounce) squares semisweet chocolate, coarsely chopped
4 (1-ounce) squares unsweetened chocolate, coarsely chopped
½ cup butter or margarine
1 tablespoon vanilla extract
⅔ cup sugar
⅔ cup firmly packed brown sugar
3 large eggs
⅔ cup all-purpose flour
¼ teaspoon baking soda
½ teaspoon salt
⅔ cup quick-cooking oats, uncooked
2 cups chocolate-covered raisins
1 cup chopped pecans or peanuts

Combine first 3 ingredients in top of a double boiler; bring water to a boil. Reduce heat to low. Cook until chocolate mixture melts; stir occasionally. Remove from heat; let cool. Stir in vanilla; set aside.

Combine sugars and eggs in a large bowl; beat at low speed of an electric mixer until blended. Beat at high speed 5 minutes. Add cooled chocolate mixture; beat well. Combine flour and next 3 ingredients; stir. Add flour mixture to egg mixture; stir until smooth. Fold in raisins and pecans. Let stand 15 minutes.

Drop dough by tablespoonfuls onto ungreased cookie sheets. Bake at 350° for 8 minutes. Let cool completely on cookie sheets. Yield: 5 dozen.

9 Chocolate Pralines

Use paper lunch sacks, a hole punch, and citrus-colored cording to make clever containers for these pecan-studded sweets.

1½ cups sugar
1½ cups firmly packed brown sugar
¼ cup plus 2 tablespoons cocoa
1 cup whipping cream
¼ cup plus 2 tablespoons butter or margarine
1 teaspoon vanilla extract
2 cups chopped pecans, toasted

Grease wax paper; set aside. Combine sugars and next 2 ingredients in a saucepan. Bring to a boil over medium heat. Boil until sugars dissolve; stir often. Cover; cook 2 minutes to wash down sugar crystals from sides of pan. Uncover and cook, stirring occasionally, until mixture reaches soft ball stage (234°). Remove from heat; stir in butter and vanilla. Add pecans. Beat vigorously with a wooden spoon 2 minutes or just until mixture is creamy and begins to thicken.

Working rapidly, drop mixture by tablespoonfuls onto prepared wax paper; let stand until firm. Store in an airtight container. Yield: 3½ dozen.

When you give these easy sauces, add a note about serving temperatures and storage (they keep in the refrigerator up to 2 weeks).

Peanut Butter Chocolate Sauce

½ cup commercial hot fudge topping
½ cup chocolate syrup
¼ cup creamy peanut butter

Combine all ingredients in a saucepan; stir well. Cook over medium-low heat, stirring constantly, until mixture is heated. Serve warm. Yield: 1¼ cups.

Bittersweet Mint Chocolate Sauce

2 (4.67-ounce) packages chocolate-covered mint wafer candies
2 (1-ounce) squares unsweetened chocolate
¾ cup whipping cream
1 teaspoon vanilla extract

Combine first 3 ingredients in top of a double boiler; bring water to a boil. Reduce heat to low; cook, stirring constantly, until smooth. Remove from heat; stir in vanilla. Serve warm. Yield: about 1¾ cups.

Orange-White Chocolate Sauce

3 (2-ounce) white chocolate-flavored baking bars
½ cup light corn syrup
¼ teaspoon grated orange rind
2 tablespoons fresh orange juice

Combine first 3 ingredients in top of a double boiler; bring water to a boil. Reduce heat to low; cook until chocolate melts, stirring frequently.

Gradually add orange juice, stirring until smooth. Serve at room temperature. Yield: 1¼ cups.

Quick Hot Chocolate Sauce

⅓ cup cocoa
¼ cup hot water
1 (14-ounce) can sweetened condensed milk
2 tablespoons butter or margarine
1 teaspoon vanilla extract

Combine cocoa and hot water in a saucepan; stir with a wire whisk until smooth. Add remaining ingredients, stirring until smooth. Cook over medium-low heat, stirring constantly, until mixture is thoroughly heated. Serve warm. Yield: 1⅔ cups.

It's a Wrap

Sheathe your chocolates in sophistication. It's easy with the gift boxes, ribbons, specialty papers, and corrugated cardboard shown in the photographs accompanying the recipes on the preceding pages. For source listings, see page 157.

Pins from the Forest

Take a hike—and gather twigs and fern fronds for these diminutive pins. Sport them singly or in multiples as wearable botanical prints.

Materials for 3 pins:
3 fern frond tips, about $^{3}/_{4}$" to $1^{1}/_{4}$" long
scrap of cardboard
scrap of parchment paper
scrap of cream textured paper
craft glue
small twigs, no larger than $^{3}/_{8}$" diameter
greenery clippers
hot-glue gun and glue sticks
3 ($1^{1}/_{2}$") metal pin backs

Note: Pins shown range from $1^{1}/_{2}$" to 2" high. For source listings for parchment and textured papers, see page 157.

1. Place fern tips between paper towels to remove all moisture; then press between pages of a telephone book (weighted with a heavy object) for about a week.

2. For 1 pin, cut a small square or rectangle ($^{1}/_{4}$" larger on all sides than fern) from cardboard. Cut 1 same-size piece from parchment and 1 from textured paper. With edges aligned, glue parchment piece to back of cardboard and textured piece to front.

3. Using toothpick, apply craft glue to back of fern. Center and glue fern to front of cardboard.

4. Using clippers, cut twigs into 4 pieces to fit around edge of cardboard. Hot-glue twigs to outside edge of cardboard. Cut 4 more twig pieces for second row. Hot-glue twigs to sides of previous row.

5. Hot-glue pin back to back of cardboard.

6. Repeat steps 2–5 to make remaining pins.

Strike Up a Bandbox

At Landis Valley Museum, Edwina Cholmeley-Jones teaches a workshop on making bandboxes the old-fashioned way. Follow her step-by-step technique to make your own decorative containers.

When Edwina conducts classes on crafting bandboxes, she uses traditional materials—pulpboard, linen thread, newspaper, and wallpaper—as well as traditional techniques. Here and on the following pages are her methods.

Materials:
patterns on page 154
tracing paper
1 sheet of 6-ply posterboard or pulpboard
wallpaper
newspaper
craft knife or sharp scissors
sharp large-eyed (#6 or #7) needle
linen thread
powdered cellulose wallpaper paste
paintbrush

Note: See sources listed on page 157 for 6-ply posterboard and linen thread.

1. Using tracing paper, transfer patterns as indicated and cut out. For posterboard side strip and rim, position long edges along the grain, so that they will curve easily without cracking, and cut as follows: For side strip, cut 1 (3½" x 18½") piece from posterboard, 1 (4" x 19½") piece from wallpaper, and 1 (3¼" x 19") piece from newspaper. For rim, cut 1 (1" x 18½") piece from posterboard, 1 (1½" x 19½") piece from wallpaper, and 1 (¾" x 19") piece from newspaper. Label all pieces.

Above: From May through October, the Yellow Barn houses workshops taught by Edwina and other craftspeople. For more on Landis Valley Museum, see the box on page 133.

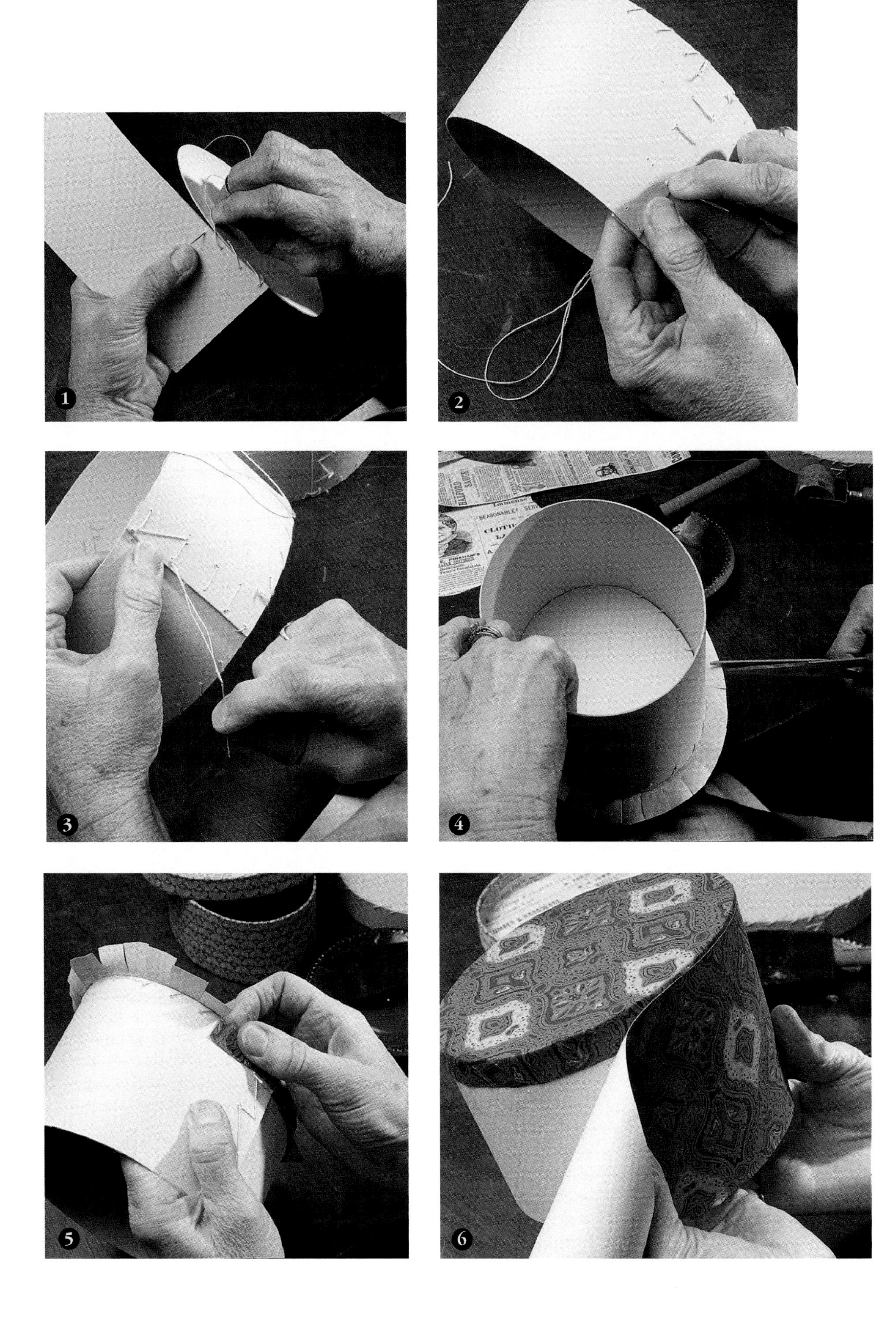
1
2
3
4
5
6

2. Construct bandbox with posterboard pieces: Place side strip around bottom of box, overlapping ends ½". Cut off extra length of side strip. Using needle to pierce posterboard, whipstitch side strip to bottom as shown (Photograph 1).

3. Stitch side seam closed with horizontal stitches (Photograph 2). Do not cut thread. Reinforce seam with diagonal stitches as shown (Photograph 3). Repeat to stitch rim to top.

4. Cover bandbox with wallpaper pieces: Mix solution of ½ ounce powder and 8 ounces water to form paste. Using paintbrush, apply a thin layer of paste to back of wallpaper bottom. Center and press to box bottom. Clip excess edges every ½" (Photograph 4). Press excess edges to sides of box, applying more paste if needed (Photograph 5).

Apply paste to back of wallpaper side strip. Align 1 edge of strip with bottom of box, allowing excess ½" to extend beyond top and overlapping ends ½". Press in place (Photograph 6). Clip excess edges and press to inside of box. Repeat to cover box top and rim.

5. Line bandbox with newspaper pieces: Paste top and bottom pieces in place first, clipping excess edges to fit smoothly. Then add side strip and rim. Let dry for 2 days.

Left: During "Days of the Belsnickle," the Landis House (foreground) is traditionally decorated in the manner of a Victorian Christmas, and the Landis Valley House Hotel (background) serves delicious holiday repasts.

Below: Mike Riordan, a museum volunteer, makes such a rascally Belsnickle that his own neighbors sometimes do not recognize him.

Yuletides of Yore

If you appreciate a little history with your holidays, head to Lancaster, Pennsylvania, and Landis Valley Museum, where a 19th-century Christmas comes to life.

Visitors to the Christmas events at Landis Valley Museum encounter a special treat. Not only do they ramble through historic buildings, peruse collections, and see demonstrations that illuminate how rural Pennsylvania Germans celebrated the holidays, but they also meet the Belsnickle.

Most of us have never heard of the Belsnickle, but for Pennsylvania Germans of the 1800s and early 1900s, his visit was as much a part of Christmas as caroling and feasting.

The Belsnickle was abroad with Santa Claus on Christmas Eve night or sometimes by himself on December 6, the feast day of Saint Nicholas. But unlike Santa, whom one never saw, the Belsnickle was very real. In each neighborhood, a resident disguised himself in tattered clothing, took up a sack of treats in one hand and a sheaf of switches in the other, and then roamed from farmhouse to farmhouse, boisterously rewarding all the children who had been good and brusquely reproaching those who hadn't. For the children, it was all good fun—as if Halloween and Christmas had been rolled into one.

Nowadays, you're likely to see the Belsnickle only at Landis Valley Museum. Every December the museum offers a program called "Days of the Belsnickle," which includes a holiday meal at the museum's 1850s hotel and a tour of three historic buildings that are authentically decorated for Christmas and enlivened by docents performing skits. At the end of the program, visitors encounter the mischievous Belsnickle.

For more information or to make reservations for the Christmas celebrations, contact Landis Valley Museum, 2451 Kissel Hill Road, Lancaster, PA 17601, or call (717) 569-0401.

THE LAP OF LUXURY

You've seen those beautiful, lap-warming fabric throws in catalogs and department stores. Why not make one and save both time and money? Unlike a quilt or an afghan, a throw can be made in an evening and for a fraction of the cost of a custom-made coverlet.

Materials:
4⅛ yards 54"-wide print fabric for backing and self-binding borders
3½ yards 45"-wide polyester fleece for lining
1⅝ yards 54"-wide print fabric for top
thread to match fabrics
8 yards ½"-diameter cording

Note: Finished size of throw is 62" square. All seam allowances are ½". For a source listing for fabric and cording pictured here, see page 157.

1. Referring to Diagram 1, cut backing fabric in half widthwise. With right sides facing, sew together lengthwise along 1 long edge. Press seam open.

2. Referring to Diagram 2, cut a 72" square from backing, centering seam.

3. Repeat Step 1 to cut and seam fleece lining. Referring to Diagram 3, cut a 62" square from lining, offsetting seam as shown to reduce bulk at center of finished throw.

4. Cut a 54" square from top.

5. Center and stack backing (wrong side up) and lining, making sure backing extends 5" on all sides. Working from center outward, baste layers together. With backing side up, stitch layers together along center seam in backing to secure lining.

6. Center top (right side up) on lining, making sure lining extends 4" on all sides. Working from center outward, baste through all layers to secure. Fold edges of backing over ½" and press.

7. To make self-binding borders, fold edges of backing over 4", overlapping top ½" and mitering corners (for step-by-step instructions on mitering corners, see page 154). Stitch through all layers ⅛" outside top square to secure borders.

8. Beginning at corner, slipstitch cording over seam. Referring to photograph, loop about 7" of cording at each corner and slipstitch in place.

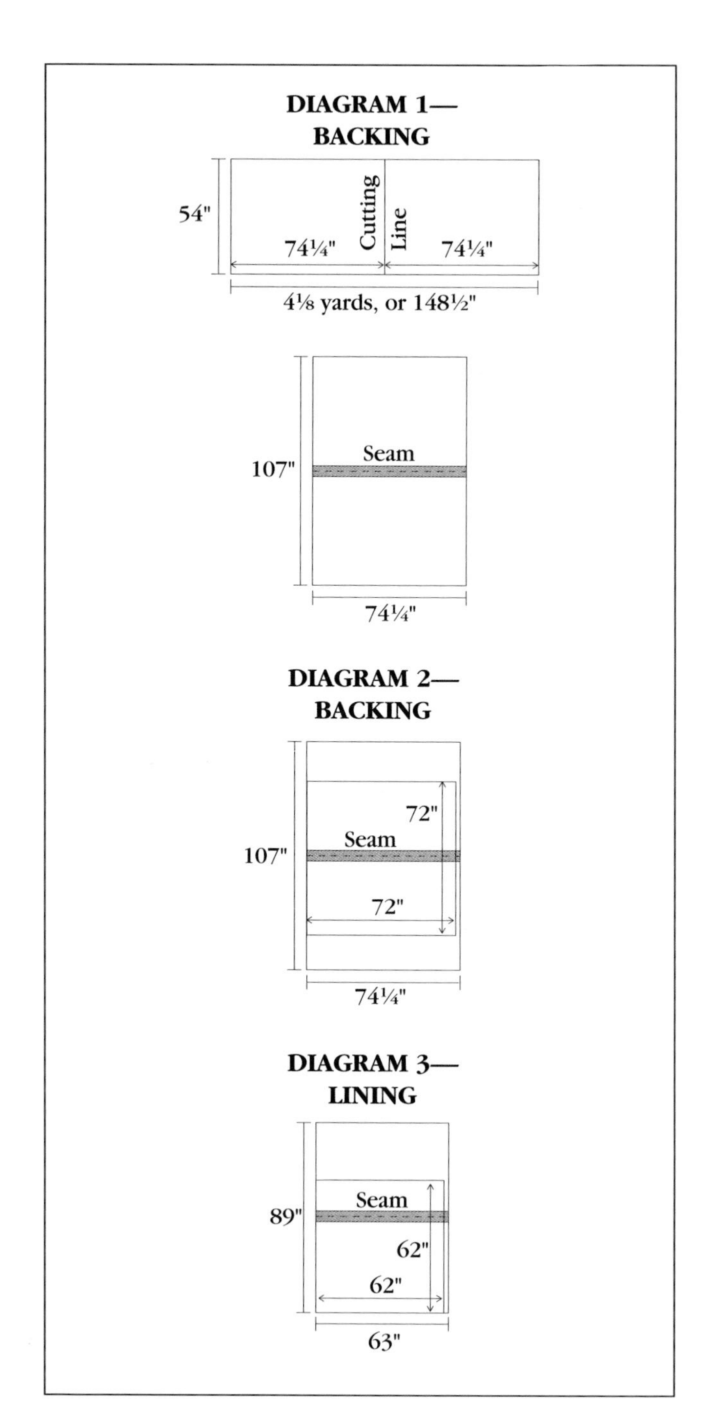

AT HOME

IDEAS

TOP-DRAWER TOPIARIES

Update your holiday decorating with seasonal topiaries that are simple to make.

You can buy topiary forms, but you'll have more options if you make your own: Insert 1 end of a stick into a Styrofoam form, and anchor the other end in a container filled with florist's foam or plaster of paris.

Most of the materials for these topiaries are found in crafts stores. For topiary forms, Styrofoam forms, crinkle wire, fresh bay leaves, and ribbons, see the source listings on page 157.

TIP: To make the Rose Globe, you can dry your own rose petals: Place three paper towels on a microwave-safe plate; arrange fresh rose petals in a single layer on top and cover with a paper towel. Microwave on HIGH for 3 minutes. Check petals for dryness; replace the paper towels when moist. Continue microwaving at 30-second intervals, checking for desired dryness.

Tiny Treasures

Spray-paint an 8" Styrofoam star green; then hot-glue small toys and ornaments to the star. Glue ribbon around the edges.

Gilded Pinecone

Paint the tips of a large pinecone gold. Spray-paint a cardboard star and a handful of Spanish moss gold. Tuck moss into the crevices of the pinecone. Hot-glue the star to the top and glue the pinecone to the florist's foam in the pot.

Star Tree

Cover a 9" Styrofoam cone with untwisted, natural-colored paper twist. Hot-glue small wooden star cutouts to the cone. Glue a star and a tiny wreath of Spanish moss to the top of the tree.

Rose Globe

Hot-glue dried rose petals (see the tip on the opposite page) to cover a 4" Styrofoam ball. Wrap crinkle wire around the ball.

Bay Tree

Pin fresh bay leaves to the bottom of a 14" Styrofoam cone. Working upward, overlap leaves to cover the cone. Hot-glue a whole nutmeg to the top.

A Tree Skirt and Stocking in the Red

Instructions begin on page 54. Patterns are full-size. Add ½" seam allowance to stocking pattern.

Note: See page 55 for Embroidery Diagrams.

Pages 52–55

Embroidery Tips

Different types of embroidery require different types of needles. For working on tightly woven fabrics such as wool or cotton, use a needle that has a sharp point, such as an embroidery or chenille needle. For cross-stitch, needlepoint, or other counted-thread embroidery, use a tapestry needle, which has a blunt point.

Work with yarns or threads cut no longer than 18"; an extremely long thread tends to knot and fray when pulled often through the fabric.

Whenever possible, use a frame or hoop. It helps keep the fabric flat and smooth and the stitches even.

Paint It Quick

For a fast alternative to traditional needle and thread, try the new dimensional fabric paints now on the market. Sold in squeeze bottles with applicator tips, they are easy to use. For a source listing, see page 157.

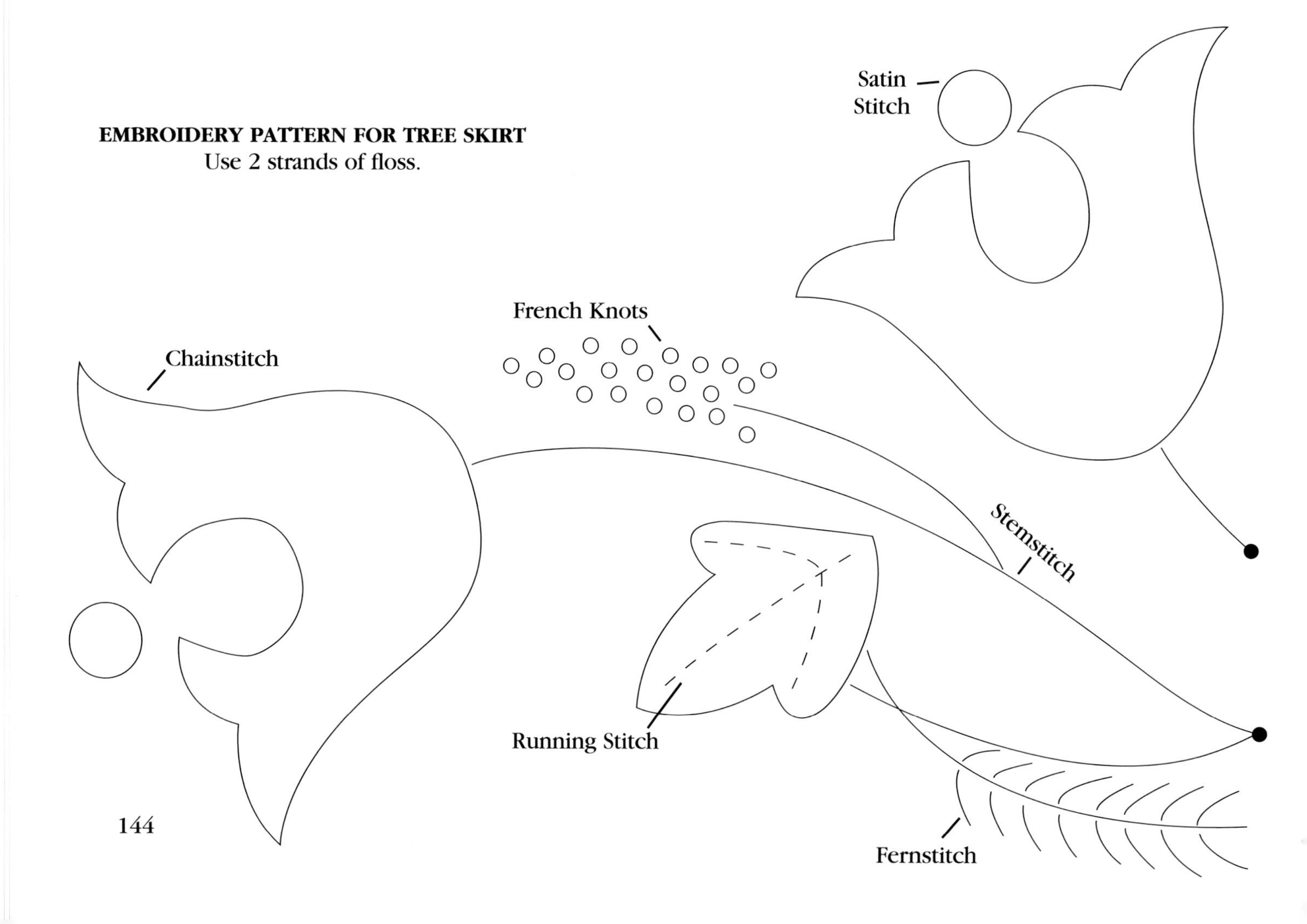

EMBROIDERY PATTERN FOR STOCKING
Use 2 strands of floss.

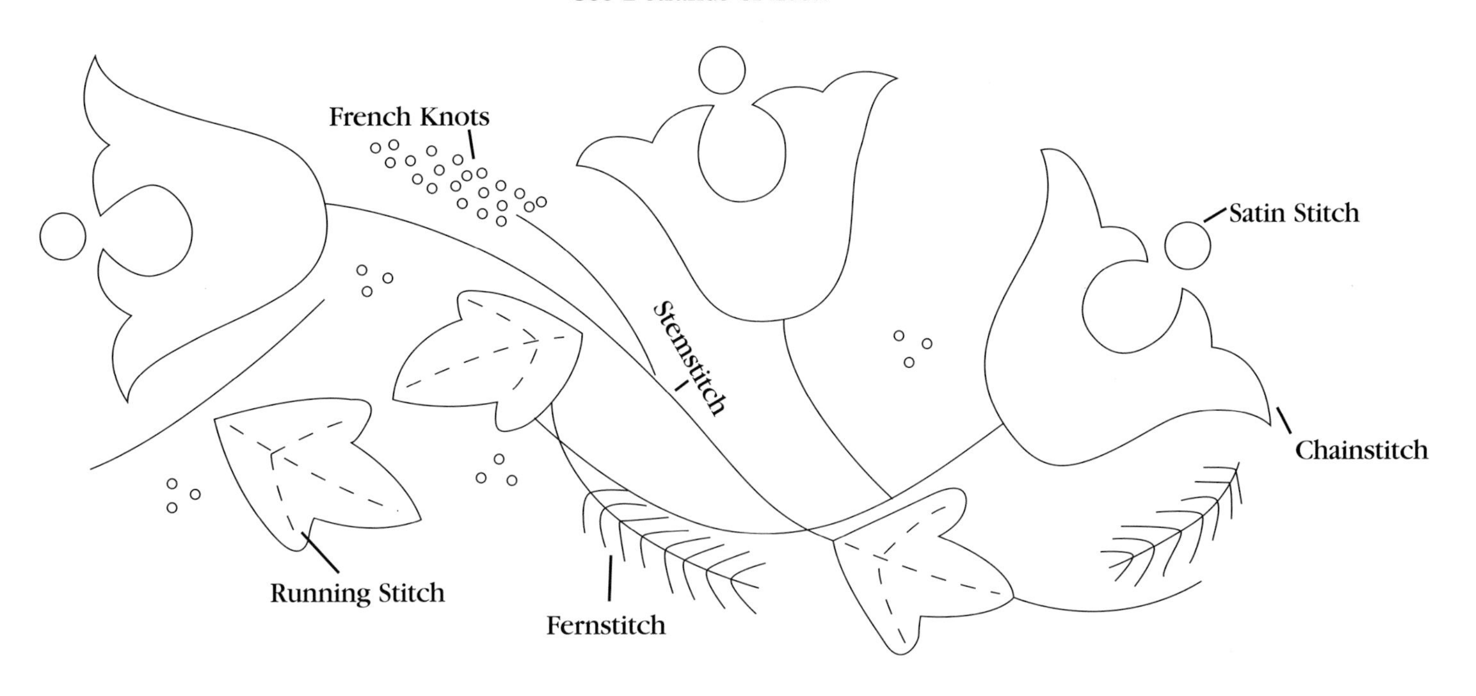

Stocking pattern continued on next page.

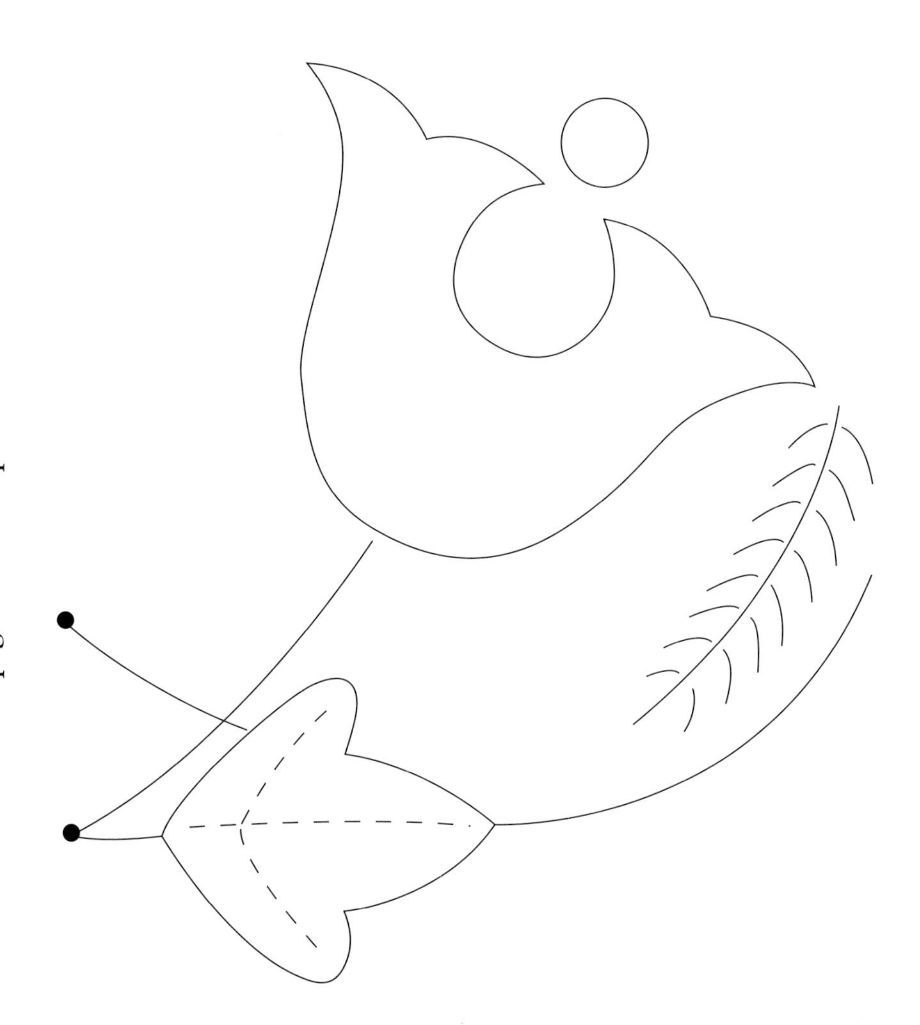

Match dots across page to connect pattern.

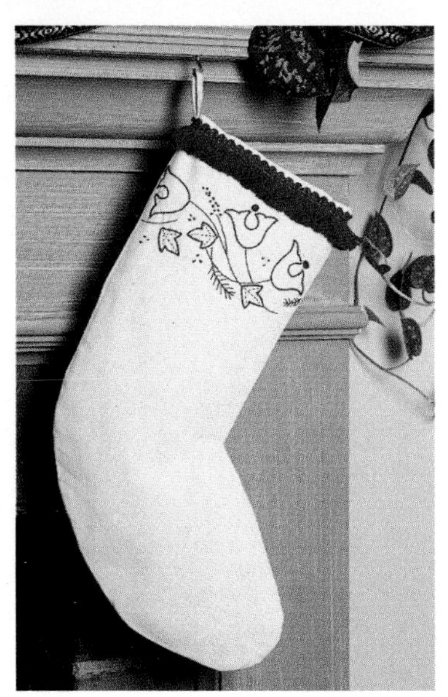
Page 53

STOCKING

Cut 4 from muslin.

Extend 7½" for complete pattern.

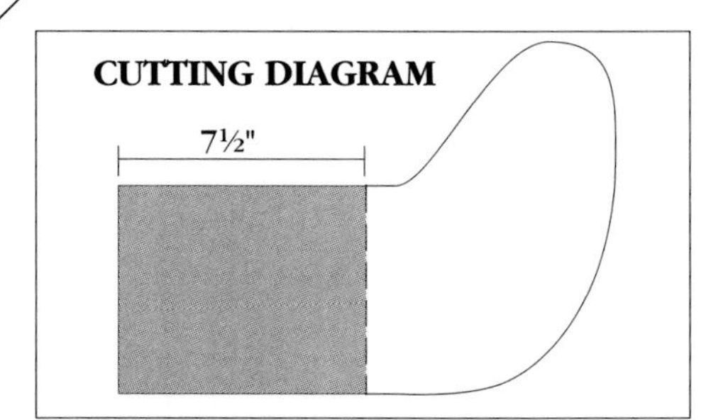

Tweedy Bears

Instructions are on page 57.
Patterns are full-size and include ¼" seam allowances.

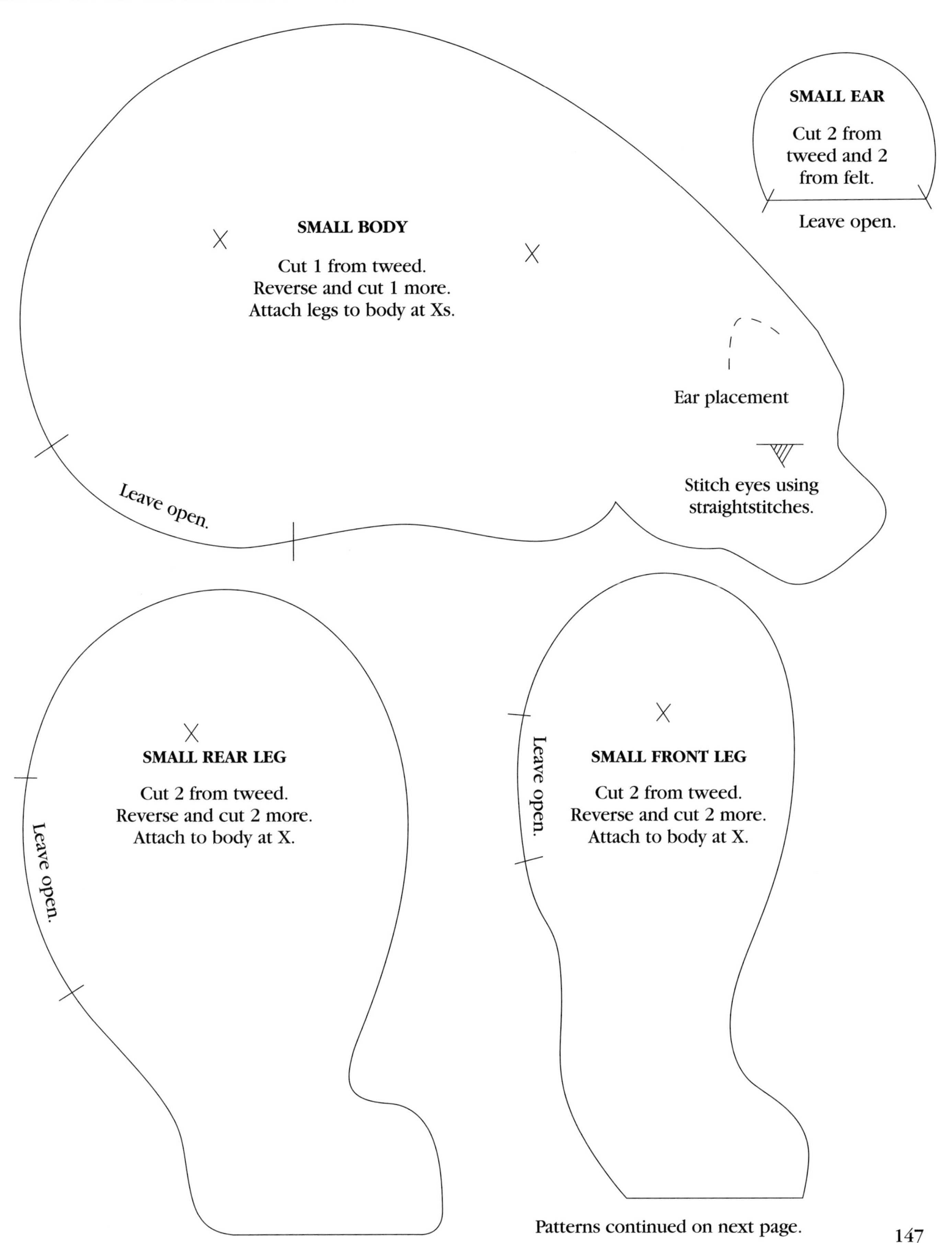

Patterns continued on next page.

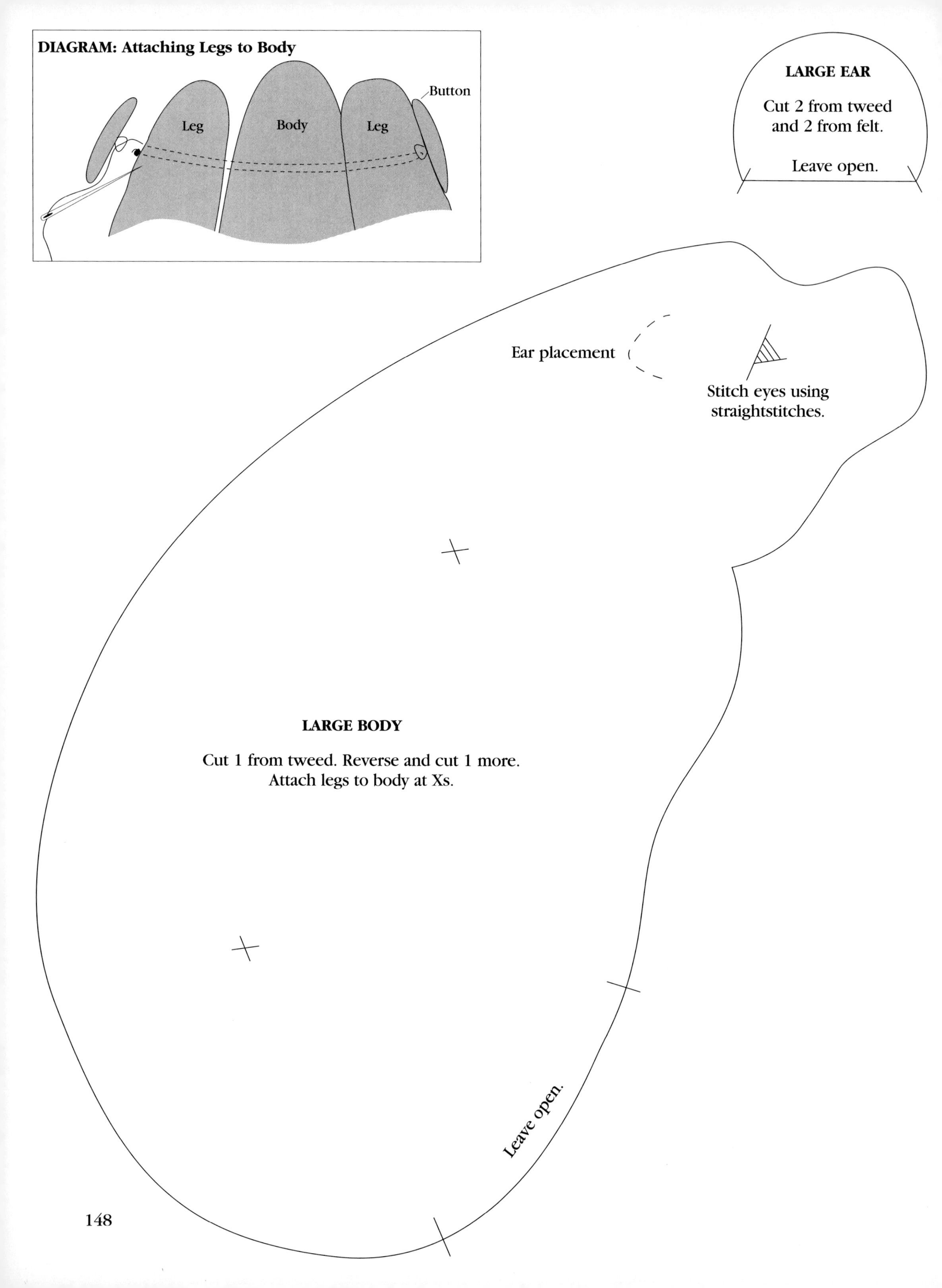
DIAGRAM: Attaching Legs to Body
Button
Leg
Body
Leg
LARGE EAR
Cut 2 from tweed
and 2 from felt.
Leave open.
Ear placement
Stitch eyes using
straightstitches.
LARGE BODY
Cut 1 from tweed. Reverse and cut 1 more.
Attach legs to body at Xs.
Leave open.

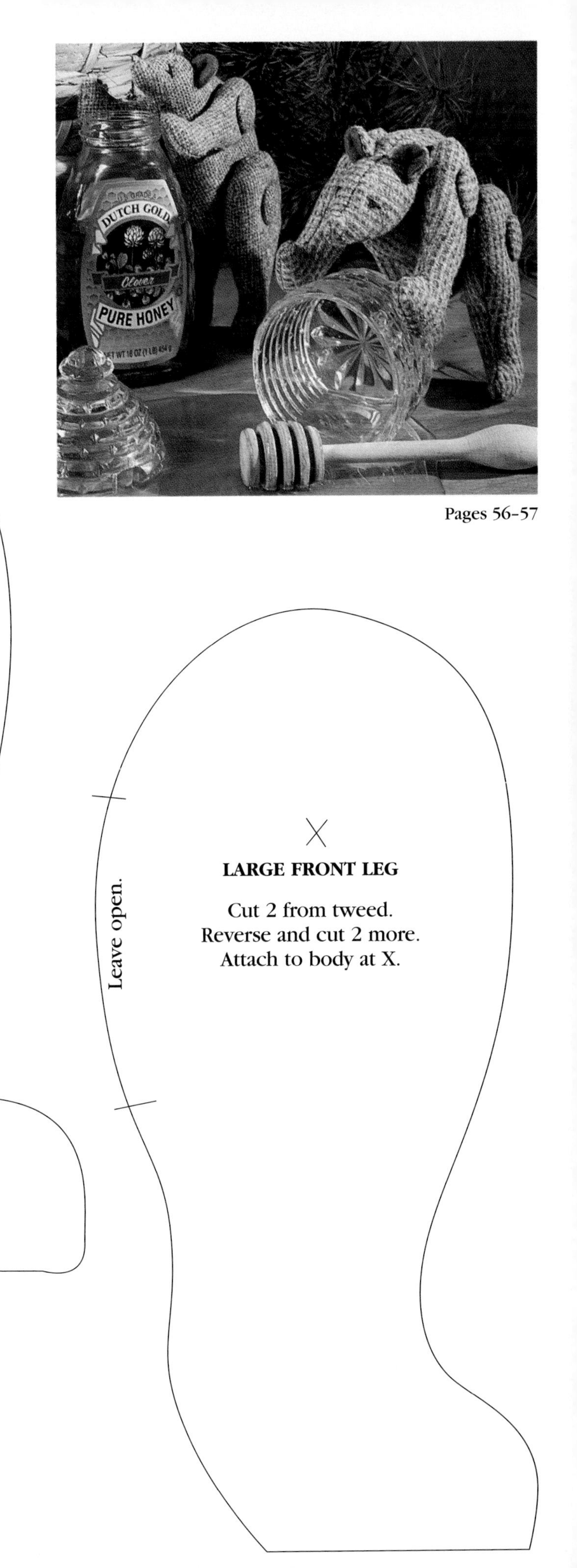

Pages 56–57

LARGE REAR LEG

Cut 2 from tweed.
Reverse and cut 2 more.
Attach to body at X.

Leave open.

LARGE FRONT LEG

Cut 2 from tweed.
Reverse and cut 2 more.
Attach to body at X.

Leave open.

Ribbon Star Ornaments

Instructions are on page 59.
Patterns are full-size.

TEMPLATE FOR 7/8"-WIDE RIBBON

Cut 6.

TEMPLATE FOR 1"-WIDE RIBBON

Cut 6.

Page 58

Beads in Bloom

Instructions are on page 49.
Patterns are full-size.

Note: Stitch beads along pattern lines, referring to photograph on page 48 for color combinations.

Fruitful Revival

Instructions begin on page 64.
Patterns are full-size. Fruit patterns include ¼" seam allowances; leaf patterns include ⅛" seam allowances.

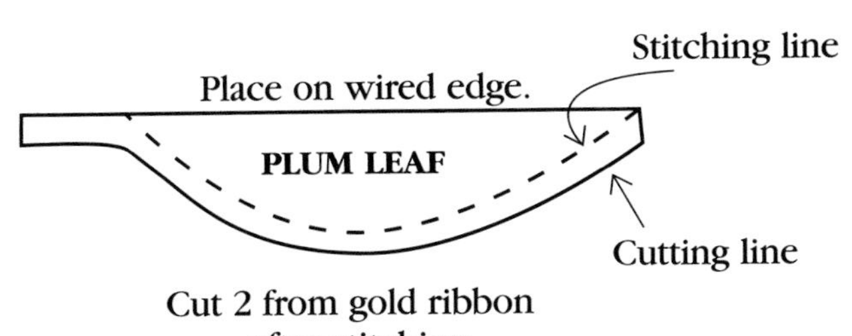

Pages 64–65

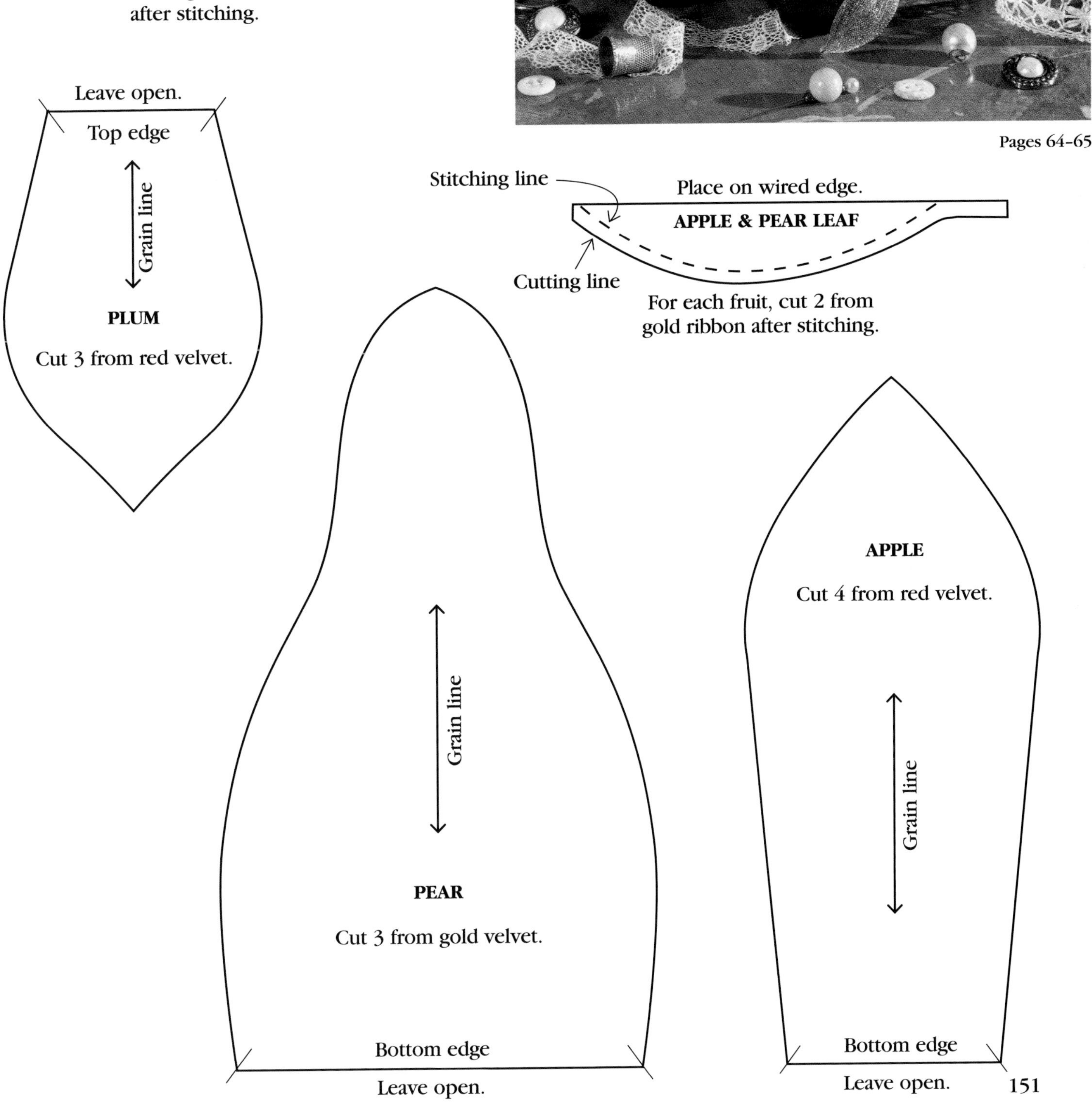

Appliqué-tions from Hungary

Instructions are on page 67.
Patterns are full-size.

By Custom Made

These three ornaments were designed by Szidor Jánosné, an artisan who lives in Debrecen, Hungary, and who sells her designs through The Sándor Collection (see pages 66–67). She is a master of cut-felt appliqué, an art indigenous to her region of Hungary. In the photograph at right, both the vest she wears and the piece she works on feature this centuries-old technique.

Whether she's making a custom bed covering for a New York designer—as she is here—or ornaments for the readers of *American Country Christmas*, Szidor uses traditional motifs, including stylized flowers, oak leaves, and wolves' teeth. The motifs can be traced back to the handsome wool coats worn by Hungarian shepherds. Today, Szidor and other local crafters use the patterns on pillows, table runners, jackets, and other decorative and wearable items.

TEARDROP ORNAMENT
Topstitch along dotted lines.
Cut along solid line with pinking shears.

DIAMOND ORNAMENT
Topstitch along dotted lines.
Cut along solid line with pinking shears.

ROUND ORNAMENT
Topstitch along dotted lines.
Cut along solid line with scissors.

Remembrance of Christmases Past

Instructions are on page 75.
Patterns are full-size.

Color Key
1 Sky Blue
2 White
3 Green
4 Dark Brown
5 Terra-Cotta
6 Red
7 Yellow

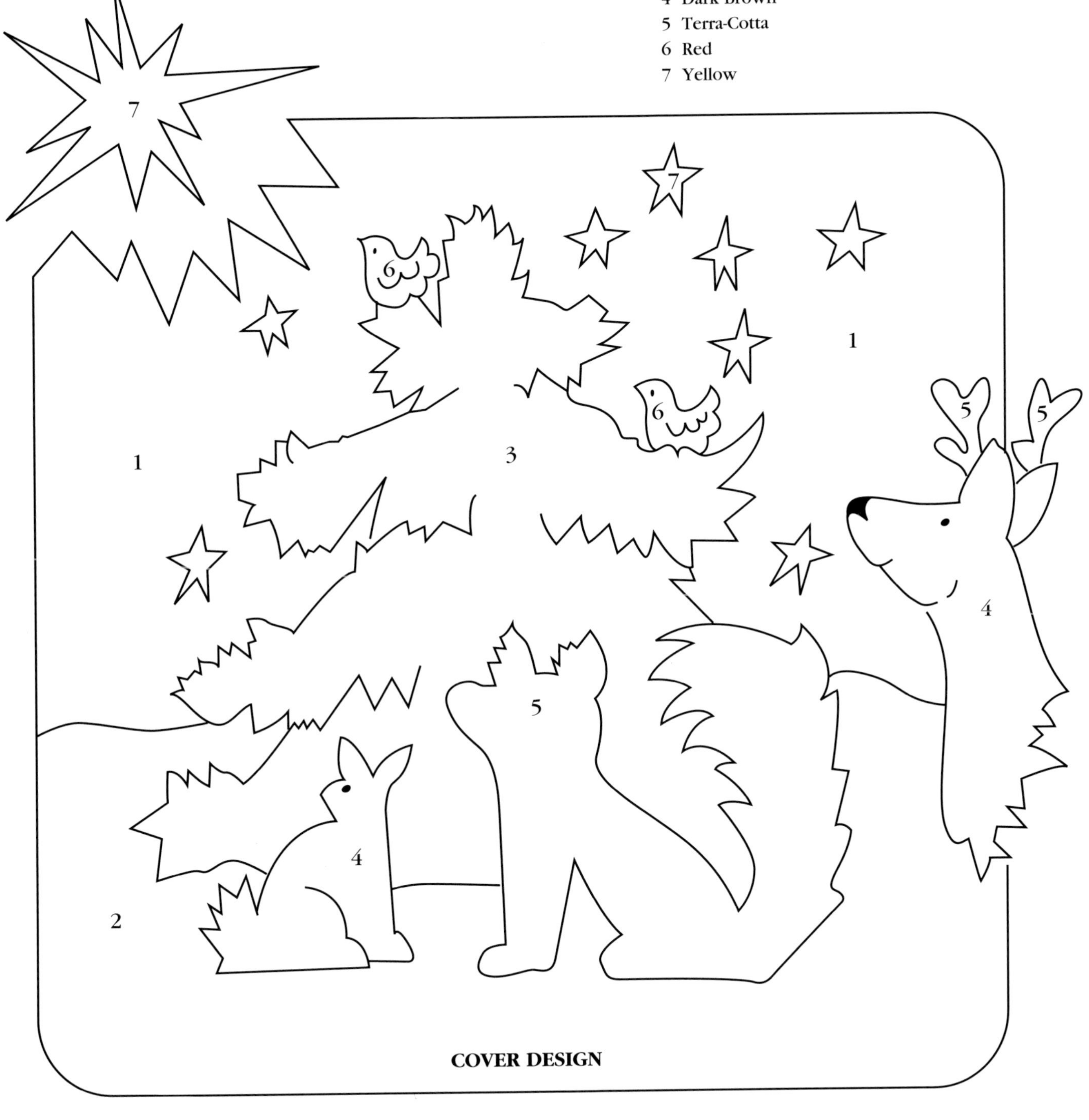

COVER DESIGN

BORDER DESIGN

Repeat border around all sides of cover design and down right sides of pages with headings.

Strike Up a Bandbox

Instructions begin on page 131.
Patterns are full-size.

BANDBOX

For bottom of box, cut 1 each on inner line from posterboard, wallpaper, and newspaper.

For top of box, cut 1 each on outer line from posterboard, wallpaper, and newspaper.

The Lap of Luxury

Instructions are on page 134.

Turning the Corner

To make smooth, professional-looking self-binding corners for throw, follow these simple steps.

Step 1. Fold edges of backing fabric over ½" and press. On top fabric, measure ½" from each edge at 1 corner and mark.

Step 2. Fold corner over so that center point on long edge of triangle aligns with mark. (Center point on long edge of triangle will be finished inside corner of miter.) Crease fold line.

Step 3. Unfold corner. Mark fabric along fold line.

Step 4. For mitered seam to show on front, fold perpendicular edges of throw together, with back of throw facing. Stitch along marked line through all layers. Trim corner ¼" outside stitched line. Unfold.

Step 5. Using a point turner, turn corner. Press corner and border flat. Repeat for remaining corners.

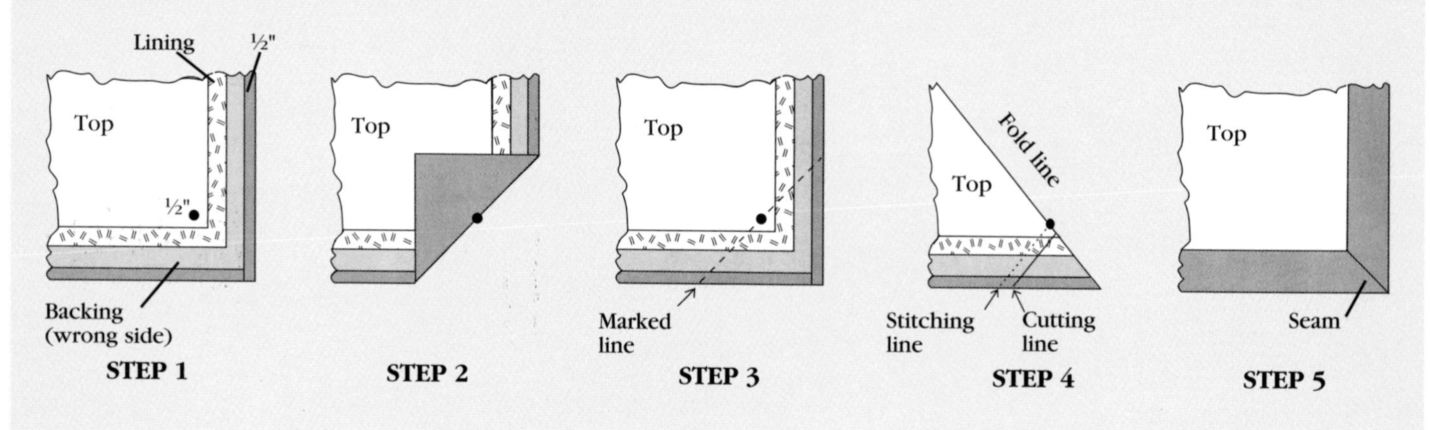

Handmade Tags in Minutes

Tennessee artist Susan Harrison designed these original gift tags to look like woodcuts.

To make the tags, reproduce this page on a photocopier, enlarging or reducing them as desired. If you like, spray adhesive on the back of the photocopied page and mount it on lightweight cardboard. While the tags are pretty left plain, you can also brighten them with colored pencils. After decorating, cut out the tags.

Make a hole in the lefthand corner or top center of each tag with a hole punch. Thread ribbon through the hole to attach the tag to your gift.

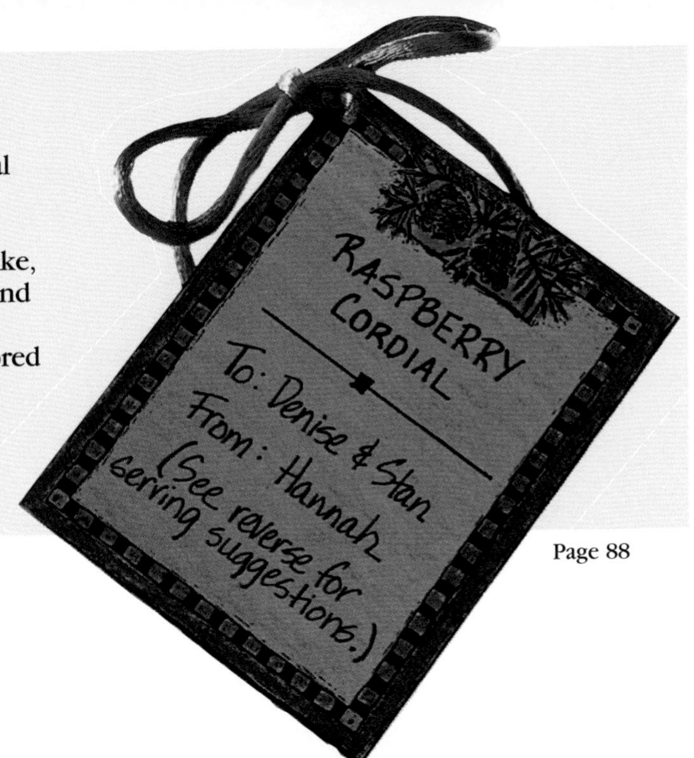

Page 88

Sources

• Page 9—unfinished, handmade wooden frames: Eisenhower's Wood Works, 80 Lake Rd., Fleetwood, PA 19522.

• Page 13—embroidery floss: Look for DMC floss at local needlework and craft stores. Or contact Craft Gallery, P.O. Box 145, Swampscott, MA 01907, or call (508) 744-2334.

• Page 18—Floralife 24-carat gold spray paint: Davis Wholesale Florist, Inc., 194 Holt Ave., Macon, GA 31204, or call (912) 742-3637.

• Page 21—Rub 'n' Buff Wax: Rub 'n' Buff, Consumer Division, American Art Clay Co., Inc., 4717 W. 16th St., Indianapolis, IN 46222.

• Page 27—Contact Elfin Glitz at 4506 Ivanhoe, Houston, TX 77027, or call (713) 629-4129.

• Page 28—handpainted Christmas plates: Contact Lindy Neuhaus Pottery, 2233 Westheimer, Houston, TX 77098, or call (713) 523-8889.

• Page 31—fresh evergreen garlands: Laurel Springs Fraser Firs, P.O. Box 85, Laurel Springs, NC 28644, or call (800) 851-2345.

• Page 37—polar fleece: Contact Frostline Kits, 2525 River Rd., Grand Junction, CO 81505, or call (800) 548-7872.

• Page 39—embroidery floss: Look for DMC floss at local needlework and craft stores. Or contact Craft Gallery, P.O. Box 145, Swampscott, MA 01907, or call (508) 744-2334.

• Page 39—gold braid: Kreinik Manufacturing Co., Inc., 9199 Reisterstown Rd., Suite 209B, Owings Mills, MD 21117, or call (800) 537-2166.

• Page 39—Aida cloth: Zweigart Fabrics and Canvas, 2 Riverview Dr., Somerset, NJ 08873-1139, or call (908) 271-1949.

• Page 39—perforated paper: For free catalog send SASE to Yarn Tree, P.O. Box 724, Ames, IA 50010, or call (515) 232-3121.

• Page 41—gift bags: Loose Ends, P.O. Box 20310, Salem, OR 97307, or call (503) 390-7457.

• Page 41—gift boxes: SIS & Sons, Inc., 428 S. Zelta, Wichita, KS 67207, or call (316) 685-6265.

• Page 43—mosaic accessories: Mary Barnett, Glass Menagerie, 3409-A Riviere Du Chien Rd., Mobile, AL 36693, or call (205) 661-5510.

• Page 51—corrugated cardboard: Contact Loose Ends, P.O. Box 20310, Salem, OR 97307, or call (503) 390-7457.

• Page 51—raffia: Loose Ends, P.O. Box 20310, Salem, OR 97307, or call (503) 390-7457.

• Pages 54, 55—embroidery floss: Look for DMC floss at local needlework and craft stores. Or contact Craft Gallery, P.O. Box 145, Swampscott, MA 01907, or call (508) 744-2334.

• Page 60—crinkle wire: Contact D. Blümchen & Company, Inc., P.O. Box 1210-OX, Ridgewood, NJ 07451-1210, or call (201) 652-5595.

• Page 61—sheer ribbon: C. M. Offray and Son, Inc., Rte. 24, Box 601, Chester, NJ 07930-0601.

• Page 61—gold-leaf kit: Houston Art & Frame, Inc., P.O. Box 56146, Houston, TX 77256, or call (800) 272-3804.

• Page 62—ribbons: For information on stores carrying Midori ribbon, call (800) 659-3049.

ribbons: C. M. Offray and Son, Inc., Rte. 24, Box 601, Chester, NJ 07930-0601.

• Page 67—wool felt: Contact Central Shippee, P.O. Box 135, Bloomingdale, NJ 07403, or call (800) 631-8968.

• Page 67—Hungarian appliqué ornaments and other crafts: Contact The Sándor Collection, 14 Johnnycake Ln., New Hartford, CT 06057, or call (203) 379-5356.

• Page 75—black photo corners: For free catalog, write Exposures, 6405 Memory Ln., Dept. 00405, Oshkosh, WI 54906, or call (800) 572-2502, Dept. 00405.

• Page 75—wave-blade paper scissors: Clotilde, Inc., 4301 N. Federal Hwy., Suite 200, Fort Lauderdale, FL 33308-5209, or call (305) 491-2889.

• Page 77—For a copy of Sandy Puckett's *Fragile Beauty: The Victorian Art of Pressed Flowers,* send $20.50 (U.S. funds only) to Victorian Art, 47 Elmwood Dr., Delaware, OH 43015.

• Page 80—specialty yarns: The London Knitting Co., 2531 Rocky Ridge Rd., #101, Birmingham, AL 35243, or call (205) 822-5855.

• Page 83—wicking and beeswax: Pourette Manufacturing Co., P.O. Box 15220, Seattle, WA 98115, or call (206) 525-4488.

• Page 86—ribbons: For information on stores carrying Midori ribbon, call (800) 659-3049.

ribbons: C. M. Offray and Son, Inc., Rte. 24, Box 601, Chester, NJ 07930-0601.

• Page 91—conchas: send $3 for catalog to Grey Owl Indian Craft Sales Corp., P.O. Box 340468, Jamaica, NY 11434.

• Page 93—jars: Williams-Sonoma, P.O. Box 7456, San Francisco, CA 94120, or call (800) 541-2233.

• Page 96—rubber stamps: Ballard Designs, 1670 DeFoor Ave. N.W., Atlanta, GA 30318-7528, or call (404) 351-5099.

• Page 97—dinner napkins: Williams-Sonoma, P.O. Box 7456, San Francisco, CA 94120, or call (800) 541-2233.

• Page 97—fabric paints: For catalog, send $3 to Home Craft Express, P.O. Box 24890, San Jose, CA 95154- 4890, or call (800) 301-7377.

• Page 100—napkins: Vietri, Inc. For store information, call (800) 277-5933.

• Page 101—votive candle holders: B.A. Evans Home House, P.O. Box 523, La Grange, GA 30241, or call (706) 882-1184.

• Page 111—seeds for everlastings: Shepherd's Garden Seeds, 30 Irene St., Torrington, CT 06790, or call (203) 482-3638.

• Page 111—dried flowers: Rosemary House, 120 S. Market St., Mechanicsburg, PA 17055, or call (717) 697-5111.

dried flowers: Contact Meadow Everlastings, 16464-CC Shabbona Rd., Malta, IL 60150, or call (815) 825-2539.

• Page 128—gift boxes: SIS & Sons, Inc., 428 S. Zelta, Wichita, KS 67207, or call (316) 685-6265.

• Page 128—ribbons: For information on stores carrying Midori ribbon, call (800) 659-3049.

ribbons: C. M. Offray and Son, Inc., Rte. 24, Box 601, Chester, NJ 07930-0601.

• Page 128—specialty papers: Loose Ends, P.O. Box 20310, Salem, OR 97307, or call (503) 390-7457.

specialty papers: For catalog, send $4 to Dick Blick Co., P.O. Box 1267, Galesburg, IL 61401, or call (309) 343-6181.

• Page 128—corrugated cardboard: Contact Loose Ends, P.O. Box 20310, Salem, OR 97307, or call (503) 390-7457.

• Page 129—specialty papers: For catalog, send $4 to Dick Blick Co., P.O. Box 1267, Galesburg, IL 61401, or call (309) 343-6181.

specialty papers: Loose Ends, P.O. Box 20310, Salem, OR 97307, or call (503) 390-7457.

• Page 131—6-ply posterboard: For catalog, send $4 to Dick Blick Co., P.O. Box 1267, Galesburg, IL 61401, or call (309) 343-6181.

• Page 131—linen thread: The Mannings Handweaving Studio, P.O. Box 687, East Berlin, PA 17316, or call (800) 233-7166.

• Page 134—fabric and cording: Osborne and Little, 65 Commerce Rd., Stamford, CT 06902, or call (203) 359-1500.

• Page 136—topiary forms: Best Buy Floral Supply, P.O. Box 1982, Cedar Rapids, IA 52406, or call (800) 553-8497.

• Page 136—Styrofoam forms: Schrock's International, P.O. Box 238, Bolivar, OH 44612, or call (216) 874-3700.

• Page 136—crinkle wire: D. Blümchen & Company, Inc., P.O. Box 1210-OX, Ridgewood, NJ 07451-1210, or call (201) 652-5595.

• Page 136—fresh bay leaves: For price list, send $2 to Bay Laurel Farm, W. Garzas Rd., Carmel Valley, CA 93924, or call (408) 659-2913.

• Page 136—ribbons: For information on stores carrying Midori ribbon, call (800) 659-3049.

ribbons: C. M. Offray and Son, Inc., Rte. 24, Box 601, Chester, NJ 07930-0601.

• Page 139—rotary-cutter mat: Clotilde, Inc., 4301 N. Federal Hwy., Suite 200, Fort Lauderdale, FL 33308-5209, or call (305) 491-2889.

• Page 144—fabric paint: For catalog, send $3 to Home Craft Express, P.O. Box 24890, San Jose, CA 95154-4890, or call (800) 301-7377.

INDEX

GENERAL

RECIPES

CONTRIBUTORS

DESIGNERS

Mary Bender Barnett,
Glass Menagerie, mosaics, 42–47.
Lula Chang,
Wooly Dreams Design, cross-stitch Santa pillow, 38–39; cross-stitch ornaments, 39.
Edwina Cholmeley-Jones,
bandbox, 130–33.
Kim Eidson Crane,
flannel nightgown, 116–17; pajama shorts set, 116–17.
Charlotte Hagood,
beaded leather ornaments, 48–49; ribbon star ornaments, 58–59; fruit-shaped pincushions, 62–65; dried-flower wreaths, 108–12.
Kenzie Hannah,
Elfin Glitz, decorating ideas, 26–29; staircase garland, 30–31.
Susan Harrison,
woodcut-inspired gift tags, 88, 155.
Linda Hendrickson,
cut-paper projects, 40–41; holiday scrapbook, 74–75.
Margot Hotchkiss,
painted napkins, 96–97.
Szidor Jánosné,
Hungarian appliqué ornaments, 66–67, 152; ornament designs brought to the United States by **The Sándor Collection**.
Marjorie Johnston,
centerpieces, 20–23; quick ideas for holiday decorating, 32–33.
Heidi T. King,
rope, twig, and seashell frames, 6–9; redwork tree skirt, 52–55; redwork stocking, 53–55.
Sandy Puckett,
pressed-flower projects, 76–79.
Meg Rice,
Elfin Glitz, decorating ideas, 26–29; staircase garland, 30–31.
Carol S. Richard,
herbal swags, 16–17; fruit pomanders, 60–61; topiaries, 136–37.
Janice Schindeler,
flavored vinegars, 113–15.
Lou Souders,
hobbyhorse, 50–51.
Gwen Swann,
woodland tablescape, 18–19.
Carol M. Tipton,
nut and stone frames, 9; pine-needle sachets, 10–12; flannel clothes hangers, 12–13; mistletoe sheet set, 12–13; tweed bears, 56–57; fern pins, 128–29.
Jonnie Venglik,
knitted mittens, 80–81; variations of knitted mittens, 81.
Cynthia M. Wheeler and Aaron Wheeler,
buffalo plaid polar fleece muffler and hat, 34–37.
Nancy Worrell,
burlap place mats, 90–91.

PHOTOGRAPHERS

All photographs except the following were taken by **John O'Hagan.**

Ralph Anderson, 9, top left 12, right 51, 60–61, 69–72, 80–81, 86–87, 92–94, background 96–97, 98–107, 112, 116–28, bottom left 130–31, 136–37.
Van Chaplin, 16–17, 20–21, top right 22, 36, 40–41.
Rick Dean, inset 6–7, inset 34–35, inset 63–64, inset 84–85, inset 108–9.
Mary-Gray Hunter, 8, bottom right 53.
Gene Johnson, 10–11, bottom left 12, 12–15.
Chris A. Little, 18–19.
Hal Lott, 26–31, 113–15.
Sylvia Martin, top right 21, bottom left 22, 23, 32–33.

PHOTOSTYLISTS

All photographs except the following were styled by **Katie Stoddard.**

Virginia R. Cravens, 69–72, 86–87, 92–94, 98–107, 118–28.
Tova Cubert, inset 6–7, inset 34–35, inset 63–64, inset 84–85, inset 108–9.
Nancy Ingram, 10-11, bottom left 12, 12–15.
Marjorie Johnston, 20–23, 32–33.
Joetta Moulden, 26–31, 113–15.

SPECIAL THANKS

• Thanks to the following talented people:

Connie Gearhardt
Nancy Harper
Carol O. Loria
Sidney Melton
Margaret Allen Northen
Barri Patton
Bonnie Scaro
Charline Sheridan
Claudia Waldron
Cynthia M. Wheeler
Denise E. York

• Thanks to the following homeowners in Alabama:

Mr. and Mrs. Leon Ashford
Mr. and Mrs. J. Brooke Johnston
Mr. and Mrs. Marshall McGarity
Mr. and Mrs. James Todd

• Thanks to the following businesses:

Annie Glass, Santa Cruz, California
Barbara Eigen Arts, Jersey City, New Jersey
Biot, New York, New York
The DMC Corporation
Dow Chemical Company
House Parts, Atlanta, Georgia
Martin & Son Wholesale Florist, Birmingham, Alabama
Surroundings, Houston, Texas
Union Street Glass, Oakland, California
Zweigart Fabrics and Canvas